1966

George F. Aschenbrenner.

CHRISTIAN MORALS

BY THE SAME AUTHOR

**THE PAIN OF THIS WORLD
AND THE PROVIDENCE OF GOD**

CHRISTIAN MORALS

BY THE VERY REVEREND

M. C. D'ARCY, S.J.

Master of Campion Hall, Oxford.

LONGMANS, GREEN AND CO.

LONDON ✦ NEW YORK ✦ TORONTO

LONGMANS, GREEN AND CO. LTD.
39 PATERNOSTER ROW, LONDON, E.C.4
CHITTARANJAN AVENUE, CALCUTTA
53 NICOL ROAD, BOMBAY
36A MOUNT ROAD, MADRAS

LONGMANS, GREEN AND CO.
114 FIFTH AVENUE, NEW YORK
221 EAST 20TH STREET, CHICAGO
88 TREMONT STREET, BOSTON

LONGMANS, GREEN AND CO.
215 VICTORIA STREET, TORONTO

Nihil obstat :
REGINALDUS PHILLIPS, S.PH.L.
Censor deputatus.

Imprimatur :
✠ LEONELLUS CAN. EVANS,
Vic. Gen.

Westmonasterii,
die 22nd JUNII, 1937.

First published 1937

PREFACE

THE first part of this book consists of addresses broadcast during the months of February and March, 1936. The subject is Christian Morality, and this was chosen because it was felt that some defence and explanation of it were overdue. Public opinion, which is beginning to be reflected in our legislation, has become impatient of many so-called conventions and the ancient code of morality. Propagandists and reformers of all sorts have been busy fostering this impatience and demanding changes more in accord, as they say, with the present outlook of society.

That certain changes are necessary is, I hope, evident to all, but the danger is that these changes should be made without any reference to the fundamental principles which govern human welfare. An apparently simple expedient may, if accepted without reflection, have far-reaching consequences and do irreparable harm to the individual and society. It will empty the baby as well as the water out of the bath. Our present troubles make us short-sighted, and we have at the present time no current philosophy of life which gives any perspective to human life and its meaning. As usually happens when a people has been robbed of a true philosophy, moral notions are settled by feeling—the most insecure of standards—sentimentalism decides immediate issues, and good and evil are identified with pleasure and pain. So it comes about that not only bad conventions are removed but fundamental moral laws are derided, and in the attempt to put pain out of sight the spirit of man is enslaved. We tend to think too little of the dignity of man and the splendour of which he is capable when roused by an ideal, and at the same time we are so sensitive to his pains and aches that we will not allow him to be disciplined at all.

Many have an uncomfortable feeling that the changes in morals which are taking place are not in the right direction, but as they have never been taught any reasonable belief they cannot suggest a remedy. That is one of the reasons why I have emphasised in the talks which follow the wisdom which has gone to the making of the Christian moral philosophy. For a number of causes into which I need not enter it has ceased to be taught, and is therefore forgotten. Rational principles are confused with Victorian conventions, and it is assumed without question by many writers to the Press and by novelists that moral convictions are bound to be relative and based on feeling. I have tried to show that the best thought of Greece and Israel and Rome is built into the edifice of Christian philosophy, and that that philosophy does give us a definite and high conception of human nature and its destiny. Once we understand man and what he can become we are in the position to lay down what is good and what is bad for him. Without such an understanding we are in the dark and what we do may wound human beings and bring about the end of our civilisation. I fear very much that this may be happening. The social theories which are now prevalent, almost without exception, misconstrue the rights and duties of human individuals and families and they lessen the sense of human dignity which every person ought to possess.

At a time, therefore, when so many are being robbed of their independence and have to live on the dole, when big business is crying for more and more efficiency, when the State is taking over the upbringing and education of the young, when all power and responsibility, if certain views come to be accepted, are to be transferred from persons to the State, it is important to consider, before all is lost, the true meaning and dignity of human persons. Our own reason should tell us that personality is something unique and sacred; the best thought of the world has confirmed this, and the Christian Revelation has shown us that each individual is infinitely precious to God with the promise before him of an immortal happiness. The broadcast talks develop this theme, beginning with the dignity of man and moving from a reasonable statement of his nature and aims to an account of what God wishes him to be.

As time did not allow me to develop a number of points which were relevant to the subject matter of the addresses, I have added several appendices. The fourth was given as a paper to a College Society at Oxford; the fifth is a summary of a paper read at Cambridge, and the last appendix is in substance an address given in Christ Church Hall at Oxford. In the broadcasts I have followed in part the line of thought developed by M. Gilson in his Gifford Lectures, The Spirit of Medieval Philosophy. The debt I owe to Mr. Christopher Dawson in my interpretation of Marx will be apparent to all who have read his book on Religion and the Modern State. The more one studies the strange mind of Marx and his inconsistencies the more is one forced to the view

worked out by Mr. Dawson, and so I have been
content to repeat in this appendix the chief point
of his analysis. I have been much helped also by
Mr. de la Bedoyère's essay, Society, in the fifth
volume of *European Civilization: its Origin and Development*, by Mr. Wood's *The Truth and Error of
Communism* and by *Essai d'une Somme Catholique contres
les Sans-Dieu*.

M. C. D'ARCY.

CONTENTS

PART I

PART II

ELUCIDATION

xi

PART I

I

THE FOUNDATIONS OF MORALITY

In *The Times* newspaper I read these words recently, which are taken from a pastoral of the Catholic Bishops of Germany: "Our German people joined the circle of leading peoples only after the Christian faith had delivered it from the darkness of heathenism and equipped it with the Christian power of grace, and will be able to walk on the high path of culture only as long as the sun of Christianity shines on it." I quote these words not as wishing to make any remark on the situation in Germany, but because they serve my purpose in talking on Christian morals. They emphasise the difference, as one of darkness and light, between heathenism and Christian life; they point to the fact, which is as true of our own as of German history, that our culture and our virtue are candles lit from the Christian torch and that with the rejection of Christian morals we may be "in an unfathomable . . . in an enormous dark drowned".

I will assume in these talks that many radical changes in morals are being suggested and seriously contemplated at the present moment. Every serious writer and every serious thinking man or woman is aware that many familiar ideas are being challenged, and not by eccentrics or small groups, but by those who have great influence and by parties which demand not so much a cleansing of the dirt and blight on our permanent beliefs in man and society as a radical change in those very beliefs. Now many of us may still think that there is no danger of such a revolution taking place, and it is usual to find the argument resting on the supposed good sense of the English character, its tenacity in holding to what is good in tradition and its refusal to be tempted to extremes. But those who think in this fashion forget that great changes can be accomplished silently and that it is by the driving in of thin wedges that the greatest masses can be broken down. In the name of desirable reforms hasty changes are made, and as their far-reaching effect is hidden—and at any rate cannot make much appeal—we, the victims of a catastrophe to come, are hoodwinked into a false comfort and retire to our beds knowing that our immediate pleasures are safe and undisturbed by the ominous bend of legislation towards barbarism.

I say "barbarism" in preference to heathenism
because there have been cultures—such as that exhibited in the Chinese exhibition—which are certainly not barbarous. We however cannot get outside our own skins; the West is permeated with the
Christian culture, and even were it not the best, as
I am sure it is, nevertheless, we cannot exchange it
for another; our fate, if we forsake it, is to fall into
savagery. That such a fate is possible history shows
only too clearly, where the jungle has crept up and
obliterated the greatest works of man and the desert
has rotted what was made in pride to defeat time.
The pessimist thinks that our western culture also
must obey the rhythm of rise and decline, but the
Spenglers forget that there is an undying grace in
Christianity and that it has in it to beautify not only
one effort of man but all which will submit to its
searchingly austere love and discipline. Nevertheless, while we may hope, there are certain conditions which must be fulfilled, and it is because they
are not being fulfilled that so many fear for our future. We have on the one hand a new morality set
forth in pamphlets and books and on many platforms,
and legislation is being bent to suit their programmes. They argue that much of our morality is
out of date, that it is based on irrational conven-

tions, that it is often inhuman and responsible for much unnecessary suffering. In later talks I will return to these challenges. For the moment I can assume that you know to what I am referring. In the novelists it is covered by the phrase "the value of experience", and in general those who wish for a change in our morals are thinking principally of the laws which touch matters of sex. The trouble however, goes deeper than that, as will be evident when I remind you that gradually a new attitude is being taken up on questions of euthanasia, suicide and private and personal rights in a State. What is praiseworthy in this campaign is the desire to lessen human suffering; what is dangerous is the reliance on sentiment and the denial of the value of principles and a firm, even inflexible ideal of man. Unfortunately those who feel that there is something incendiary in this new morality seldom pride themselves on possessing rational grounds for opposing it. As in religion so in morality its defenders are content to hand over to the opposition the weapon of reason and turn to some inner feeling and assurance. Not that the opposition has reason on its side. Far from it. What happens is that the conservative side get angry and chide, and the reformers grow still more angry and stir up an even stronger counter sentiment for their side by quoting hard cases and drawing piteous pictures of the suffering caused by rigid principles. Such misty combats can never end in truth, and it is for this reason that I wish in this first talk to say something about the foundations of morality. Without having a fairly clear idea of human nature and its end and object and then of its reasonable demands, our understanding of Christian morals will be left hanging in the air. Christianity is first and foremost a religion and not a moral code. In what concerns morals it turns first to the truths which belong to man as man and are applicable to him in any mature civilisation, be it Confucian, Socratic or Christian. What the Christian faith and grace can do with these truths will be explained later.

As I have said, in the present dispute about morals both sides tend to take for granted that the issues can be decided without any reference to human nature. Some of the new moralists, indeed, hold, so far as I can see, philosophic views which make their moral enthusiasms hard to understand; for if man be not free, if he be a creature of instincts or galvanised into activity by glands or unconscious or economic factors, there seems no reason why there should be all this shouting in the market-place about what cannot be helped. Others who never give a thought to whether man has but a short span of years and then extinction or an immortal happiness in store for him seem quite sure they know what is the best thing for him to do now. For my own part I am sure I would behave quite differently if I thought this universe had no author, and that behind nature there lay nothing but a blank inane. That is to say, we are arguing very unreasonably if we take morals as quite independent of our general view of ourselves and the purposes of the universe. I once heard a speaker argue that if we do not know what a thing is for we are likely by meddling with it both to damage ourselves and to damage it; and he gave as an example a savage who picks up a razor and first cuts his finger with it and then having experienced its sharpness decides to use it for cutting his wood. Not knowing the razor's purpose he damages both himself and it. This argument can be pressed too far,* because we are so endowed by reason that we can normally distinguish between good and evil or what is morally right and wrong. I say "normally" because our human constitution is such that we can be easily misled by trusting to our spontaneous reactions in moral matters. Why this is so I will try

* cf. Note A, p. 18.

8

to explain, as it brings us close to the main theme of these talks. When we call an action right or wrong we take for granted that the action really is right or wrong and that it is not just a matter of our individual taste, as when we like strawberries with mustard.

The majority of wise men in every age have ranked moral judgment with scientific judgment; that is to say, they put goodness and truth together as the province of the mind and not the senses. It is clear, however, that feelings and emotion enter far more into morality than into science. They are not absent from science, for without interest a scientist will not progress far, and he never ceases to be human. (This the loves and quarrels and pride of scientists have plainly shown.) The subject matter of science is nevertheless cold and abstract, whereas the subject matter of morals is one which stirs the desires and emotions of man. What a man notices and what he does in conduct is not seen through a telescope; it is not a subject for cataloguing in a museum; it touches him to the quick, and it is greeted with approbation or disapprobation in varying degrees. Hence there is a whole range of moral emotions which we know of as attached to the common virtues and vices. The obvious conclusion I would have you draw from this is that moral judgments are a mixture of thought and emotion, or better that our realisation of right and wrong are accompanied and supported and heightened by feeling and emotion and sentiment.

The second fact about moral judgments to be noticed is that they appear to be the commands of our reason, and that is why we speak of the law of conscience. They have a gravity often out of all proportion to the circumstances. A lie or dishonourable act may be unimportant in its consequences; it will soon be forgotten and lost in the myriad events which are swept away by time, but in another sphere outside of time it remains an outrage. The seamless garment of goodness has been torn, something virginal has been tarnished and not all the perfumes of Araby can cleanse the stain. This is what the moralist Kant meant when he compared the moral law to the starry heavens. The laws of morality embedded in our nature are as it were an echo from on high; they belong to a world which is timeless and unchanging, the world which Plato called "yonder", the realm of mind and spirit.

Take now these two characteristics of morals, and you will find that the history of morals confirms their truth while they in turn explain much in the

history of man. We are constantly told that morals
are relative, and for proof of this the odd customs
of various tribes and ancient peoples are quoted to
us. It is easy to exaggerate this variety of custom,
and I would have you notice the astonishing agreement amongst the sages and thinkers of every age,
the amount which the Chinese and Indians and
Arabs and Greeks have in common, and the family
likeness between the highest moral heroes of every
age. In the light of this agreement it is not too difficult to explain the variety. If moral judgments are
weighted with emotions, then by playing on the
emotion it will be easy to pull the mind to agree
with it. When we have a grievance how prompt we
are to find apparently good reasons to justify it, and
is there any other explanation for the fierce disputes
between family and family, class and class, political
faction with political faction and nation with nation?
This rationalising, as the psychologists call it, is going
on all the time, now as much as in past ages, and
moral judgments are twisted by passion to support the
persecution of inoffensive persons, the breaking of
treaties, sweated labour and a whole mumbo-jumbo
of superstition. The godlike mind has been suffo-
cated by the smoke of passion, or dulled by association and suggestion. Call religion the opium of the

people, and the pleasant turn of the words with their semblance of reason will suffice to make numbers of people swallow the saying. Where then does the so-called relativity point? Surely to the truth of human nature, that man is half spirit and half matter, that he is nevertheless one in some mysterious way, that the secret of his life is to have a perfect poise between the demands of these two lives in him, and that this poise consists in disciplining the lower part of his nature to the needs of the higher. At the beginning of history it is natural to find the mind more in fetters to the feelings, even as children are carried away by their feelings and imagination, but as experience gathers wisdom and the wise begin to direct, so do we see the image of perfection purify itself and the soul of man begin to direct its activities to an immortal enterprise. The conflict however continues between the spirit and the flesh, the unstable feelings and the unchanging knowledge of the mind, and on the success of one or the other depends the issue of civilisation or barbarism.

The same truth is illustrated by the history of conscience. Conscience must be erect and clear-sighted. It claims to be absolute, and it is a perpetual reminder to us and admonition that we must "hitch our waggon to a star", "dress our days to a dexterous and starlight order", stand firm by "a light which was never on land or sea" though the heavens crack and we gain the whole world in losing our soul. And yet it is invaded by feeling and passion and we can develop a false conscience and commit great wrong in its name.

If then we would reform our morals, we must exercise the greatest caution lest we fall into the same errors which have stained and destroyed other peoples and civilisations, and to move securely we must watch the interplay of the different forces in man and have a clear understanding of his purposes and nature. There are two conflicting tendencies in man. The one finds satisfaction in the life of colour and sound, all that makes experience warm and near to us; the life of the body and of the emotions and instincts, with their momentary delights and their swift passing. This swift animal life, which when employed properly, is so necessary for our full life on earth, tends when out of control to a kind of jazz tune, a restlessness and boredom combined. It is responsible for the constant change of fashion in clothes and popular songs and novels and the daily newspapers, in holidays and food and drink and the desire for change even in government and art and morals. On the other side of human nature is a desire for absolute knowledge, for rest from the sensuous, for calm and peace, the abstractions of the sciences and mathematics and philosophy, for a vision of perfect beauty and goodness. We might think that it is here that the true life of man consisted, but there is a cold wind which blows around its borders, and the results of abstract thinking are like the coffins of the Escurial, majestic and lifeless.

The true poise between these two tendencies has troubled the ages. They come together as it were by accident in a moment of a civilisation, and then great exploits are flashed off and man becomes truly man for a short while. Philosophers have sought to establish the true connection and devise an end for man which would harmonise all that is in human nature. Time and time again moralists have failed, but there is one wisdom which forms the ground-work of Christian belief which has successfully united these strands and therefore taught a morality which is unfailing. Unlike the extreme Platonist and what has been called, I know not with what truth, the Puritan, Christian morality has not taught that the flesh is evil and the life of the senses necessarily a vanity. Unlike again the Hedomist it has not taught that pleasure is the all in all of life. It has

found a divine poise, both because it has turned to
the Alpha and Omega of life, the Source of Light
and End of man, and because it has integrated all
that goes to the make-up of man into one splendid
conception. The great contribution of the Jews to
morality, embodied in the Ten Commandments
given to them by God, their austere sense of duty
and the law and high destiny, the philosophic understanding of life and its balanced harmony taught by
the Greeks, the social order which the Roman in
his strength fostered, these and many another ex-
pression of man's nature and genius were woven into
the Christian moral ideal and transformed by the
coming advent of the living God to dwell amongst us.
What is vital to us as it has been to every age is to remember that only when the instincts and passions of
man are tranquillised and set in order by the logos,
and in turn when the logos is lit up from within by
the love and the wisdom of God, can men and
women live truly and love truly and reach that peace
which has been defined as the tranquillity of order.

What I have been saying is a preface to a talk on
Christian morals, necessary, I believe, because we
are rapidly losing our sense of the nature and dignity
of man, and because we are ignorant of the august
history, the wisdom which from Hebrew and Greek

and Roman and down the centuries has gone to the thinking out of what is the Christian moral. It is a philosophy of life which has created the best in our culture and has sufficed to make the masterpieces of the saints and heroes whose names are familiar to us from childhood. Without the clear Greek and Christian teaching on the relation of the mind to and its control of our feelings we thoughtlessly will unleash the latter and find ourselves back in barbarism, and unless we supplement the Greek teaching of the supremacy of mind by the Christian knowledge of man's dependence on God, the spirit of man will relapse into that pride which is the arthritis of the soul. Man when he gazes at himself soon loses all knowledge of what he is really like, and the maddest views become the fashion of the day. The man whom Christianity knows is neither God nor beast, nor hedonist nor stoic, nor sexless nor sex-mad. He is a goodly, poor fellow who is plagued with good as well as bad dreams, with a sense of incompleteness which all his successes and failures serve but to confirm. He is for ever chasing himself to catch his own shadow; he swings between a worship of himself as God and a disgust at his own limitations. He rushes to indulgence and despises himself for his own weakness; he swears fidelity and cannot keep

16

his vow; he preaches peace and is his own worst enemy; he plans for all time and dies that others may reap. This is the man who peers out of history and is known by every one of us in the silent moments of the night, and it is this creature who has the majestic canons of morality to observe and the exacting duties and ideals of which I will speak next time.

NOTE A

I do not deny that most men and women are so
endowed by nature that they can distinguish good
from evil, a just deed from an unfair one, honour
from dishonour, without a profound knowledge of
God or of their souls. Indeed their readiness to hate
vice and act decently is just where they show their
paces, and bear witness to what they really are. Such
conduct judges them, as litmus paper tests the
chemical. But unfortunately, as I have already said,
our moral sense is very soon warped, and we begin
to entertain all manner of strange and freakish notions. We are far more dependent on our beliefs
than we imagine. Make money your God and you
will in time think of others as nothing but machines
to make your fortune, and unconsciously your treatment of them will become thoroughly immoral.
Lose faith in your own freedom and you will excuse
weaknesses of your own and in time think nothing
of them. Ignore God and the horizons of this life
will close in on you till you think without check of
how you can spend it in enjoyment. You will regret
too many children, you will think the old age of

others an encumbrance and your main thought will be to increase the pleasure of yourself and others and do away with pain at all costs. This means that there will be no hesitation in making the end justify the means, that you will be fretful in face of any pain whose utility is not immediately obvious and that you will measure wrongdoing and vice entirely by their consequences in affecting the happiness of the world around you.

The trouble is that many feel so strongly now whenever a chance of preventing or lessening pain is concerned that it is impossible to bring them back to principles; mention war or childbirth or even blood sports and discussion flies out of the window to make room for sound and fury. For the moment I am not dealing with these vexed questions. My point is that unless you have a clear idea of life and your place in it, you will be at the mercy of senti-ment and passing fashion. You will be like a tailor who cuts his cloth to suit the latest style without any knowledge of the shape of the human body. Do let us get the shape of the soul of man. I maintain that you cannot do this without a moral doctrine which embraces the soul, immortality and God. Once that has been done satisfactorily we can talk of Christian morals.

NOTE B

We have to face the general difficulty that morals do appear to change, and there are the special difficulties of our own time and the many, as I think, false means suggested to solve them. Let me begin with the former. There is no doubt that manners and morals have changed in various times and places. I need not weary you with examples. Now this variation would be disturbing were we to find such violent contrasts in principle as well as in detail and nothing comparable or common. But so far from this being the case we find wherever the wisest of a nation or culture have sat down to teach and write about morals there is a remarkable agreement. I remember not long ago some Chinese scholars telling me that the oldest and best in Chinese tradition bore great similarity to the oldest and best in the West, and you have only to think of the wise sayings you have heard from India or China or Africa to notice how close to our own hoarded wisdom they are. In other words, just as you find in the Indian and Arabian and Greek and German philosophies the same preoccupation with a few fundamental issues, such as the nature of God and man and the relation between them, and between time and permanence and sense and thought, matter and spirit, so will you discover by browsing amongst the great moralists and the great moral codes of man that they have appreciated the same problems and approached the same answers. But between the reflected wisdom of the great minds and the practices, whether in religion or morals, you will certainly observe a difference. Yes, and the reason is easy to find. This so called relativity of morals is a bogy and it can easily be explained without leaning on scepticism. Grant that each man is made up of body and mind, that he has physical cravings and that his feelings and emotions are like treacherous cats, ready to follow anyone who pets them and indulges them. Grant, too, that men and women take a long time to learn, and that ages can be compared to the transition from childhood to maturity. Then is it not obvious that we must expect vagaries of practice and custom and growth through experience? The fact therefore that men at various times have varied their morals is not an argument for their relativity; it is rather a proof of the one human common nature of all men and one absolute standard and ideal. The main errors arise from childishness and when passion is in the saddle; the young so easily admire strength and the qualities conspicuous in the gods of Olympus and Valhalla; and not only the young but the old as well let their feelings and desires sway them and then call what they desire admirable.

In the search for truth, in the sciences and philosophies, love of novelty, boredom and envy and pride of discovery and laziness have played havoc and make history so sadly chequered and sadly human, and yet in science the object of search is comparatively cold and unemotional. Whereas the objects of morals, the right and the good, are inseparable from emotion. We estimate facts and esteem or reprobate conduct. That is to say that the feelings and emotions and passions are alive and tumultuous when it is a question of deciding what is fair and what is evil, and moreover these feelings can be excited out of all due proportion by physical needs and conditions. Hence it is to be expected that human life should show a continual reel to the circumference in its habits and return with difficulty to the centre. Let there be economic necessity, and what is valuable will tend to be dictated by it; that is the partial truth in the saying that morals rest on economics. If women are scarce, or flocks or gold, they become rare, and their worth may be so extolled as to seem divine. Let the life of a small community be endangered by foes and dissension within, then order may be regarded as a divine ordinance. Always can we trace the origin of excess and defect and this personal equation, so to speak, can be corrected. Each age has its temptations, ours no less than others, and we have to look for the false weights in morality in what seems very near and dear to us. That is why for a serene and true understanding of morals we must ever beware of those who tell us that we must be up to date, that our morals must fit the troubles and difficulties which plague us. There are, of course, problems peculiar to every age which require attention, but when we are told that our morals must be cut to suit our present needs, it is nothing but the old barbarism disguised. A new morality is up to date by harkening to an ephemeral passion instead of abiding in the wisdom of principles which cannot change. Like the loving bear in La Fontaine which would save its master's rest by hitting the fly on his nose with a paving stone this age kills to cure, and by focussing its attention on one particular object does precisely what the authors of the strange aberrations in ancient religion and morality did. To be fair I must add that those who oppose them also, alas, make the same error. They fasten on to some indefensible part of the code they like, protest against any change and are as stupid in their obstinacy as any savage worshipping a stock or stone.

Here is the explanation of the so-called relativity of morals. By our nature we are fickle and ready to listen to the mob of our desires; we mix delusion with truth and are dazzled by imitation ideals, and once we have accepted the error or imitation we make laws and customs about it and are with the greatest difficulty freed from our prejudices. What then is the pilgrim's way to the temple of goodness and righteousness? You may expect me to answer in two words, Christian morals, and perhaps you have been wondering at my slow approach to them. But even now I must delay, and it is rather in what I have already said that I would suggest the answer to my question. Our judgments of what is good for us and others are blown upon by all the winds of feeling and passion, and our only defence against them is to have some power within us which can be like a fixed star in the sky high above passion and able to guide us. These uncontrolled desires, this short-sightedness, are our danger, and surely it is in the direction of reason that we must look. Reason can look before and after; it is the one light of truth within us; it can cast that light upon the longings and habits which tempt us; its judgments are drawn from what is immutably true, and so it can rule without fear or favour to the passing whim or difficulty. Moreover, reason makes a moral code to be enlightened, and sets it in its proper perspective. Yet even when we use our reason we can do so short-sightedly by not taking into account all the factors and circumstances. You know how many plans of parents and schoolmasters and employers and states-men and reformers, moral and religious, are wrecked by their lack of knowledge of human nature. There are a number of writers to-day who are busy telling us how and why we ought to behave, but very rarely do they stop to tell us what they think of man and human nature. To judge from what they say in asides, often enough they do not seem to believe that we know anything about human nature, and they have grave doubts whether we have souls or free will and whether we have any life beyond the grave. In other words they would prescribe for man without knowing his story or any of the chief facts about him. This seems to me to be madness. How do they know that they are not doing more harm than good? It surely makes a vital difference whether a man is to be treated as an animal or higher

25

than an animal, whether he is capable of improving himself freely or is the outcome of his time and place, whether justice or chance rule the earth and death swallow up all ambitions. If I were assured that cats and dogs had unending life and that their status in the next world were dependent on their conduct in this I would behave very differently to them; if again I thought that each were a special creation, a unique facet of eternal beauty, I would treat each with reverence and watch over its welfare with a new regard. Yet we frame moral codes without any concern for such vital matters. Think what a difference mortal or immortal life makes to our attitude to pain, or again what a vastly different complexion is put upon an evil act of ours if it affect not only ourselves but others, and again not only others but one who is author and end of our life, closer to us than hands and feet, one in whom we have our being! Supplement this last by adding that he who is our beginning and end is also the prime mover of all love, its fountain whence spring all the fleeting drops which water our dry lives—and we can begin to have some idea of the need of a true understanding of ourselves and nature before we close the book of morals.

II

DIGNITY AND PERSONALITY

In my last talk I said something about the grandeur of the Christian view of life and its influence on morals. Now, many men do not bother about what they will call these high and obscure questions, and will say, "I try to live an average decent life and do my job if I have one." Others may say, "I try to be kind to others and I have never heard of anything better than that." Let us grant that most people we meet are good and capable of much simple heroism and generosity. The War proved that. But that is not to say that we can do without a high moral code and ideal. We take our opinions from those around us and are influenced willy nilly by prevalent ideas. We may believe in them consciously and proudly or we may adopt them unconsciously. It is far better as a rule to believe than to suspend our judgment or give up all faith. I say as a rule because the kind of belief or faith which is stirring some countries at present has produced many absurdities and many horrors. To believe in breed to such an extent that you must bully supposedly inferior breeds without the law is shameful; here a false belief directly affects the morals of its adherents and lowers them. On the other hand, nothing worth doing will be done by those who have no faith. The lounger, the nuisance who is satisfied with fault finding and criticising every proposal, Mr. Hum and Haw who can never take sides, none of these will make much of a Jerusalem in England's green and pleasant land. Those who gain the prizes of life or leave their mark for good or evil have always believed either in their talent or themselves or fate or some crusade or God. But woe to the disillusioned; they have no hope, and they become the prey of the ruthless or fall sick with all the epidemics of their age and time.

It is this danger of succumbing to a number of quack remedies and losing all human dignity to become robots or the slaves of instinct and natural conditions which is besetting us now. The blood of the War estranges us from the nineteenth century. The current of thought of that century was idealistic. It started with the belief that man had only to be freed from all restrictions to enter into his kingdom; the individual must enjoy full liberty, the voice of the people must be heard in the State and be accepted as the voice of God; trade must be free and economic competition must bring prosperity; science will open up the earth to be a paradise and evolution will show the way to a perpetual progress; and these views were embodied in an idealistic philosophy which declared man to be the procession of God's thought in time, the veritable God, mistaken as aloof and transcendent in times past and now manifested in the actions and thoughts of democracy, and most properly in the State, which can therefore do no wrong. This belief, as happens with all beliefs, produced many great men and great achievements, but its falsity was exposed in the War and its nemesis is upon us now. With bitter irony the children of that age, the divine come upon earth forsooth, found themselves massacring one another and the federation of the world a shambles.

The War seemed then a mockery of the old idealism, and so the post-War generation has tried to wipe that idealism out of its mind, and either because each man kills the thing he loves or because he likes to cut off his nose to spite his face, he looks with favour now upon all ideas which spit at man's greatness.* Most philosophers, *de nos jours*, do not

* With the hate that you're so rich in
  Light a fire in the kitchen,
  And the little god of hate, turn the spit, spit, spit.
  A. HUXLEY.

29

trust anything but sensation; we are told that all man's activities are summed up in the words "animal behaviour", or that our conscious life is the slave of the unconscious; we dance to the tune of some hidden libido or harken automatically to the repressed voice of our childhood; and if this does not suffice we can always say that desires and actions are determined by the economic demands of the time. Thus does the street arab pull snooks at the lifeguardsman and Everyman find rest from bad dreams by watching the happy antics of Mickey Mouse.

Of course there are masses of decent people who have no use for this degrading humbug, but they cannot escape pessimism among the shadows cast by past and present follies. They have been shaken out of security by the economic depression, and they feel the steady encroachment of scientific invention on individual craft and workmanship. The moving staircase of modern life muddles the mind, and the young with no outlet for their energies and no repose of soul are huddled against street corners or saving pennies for cinemas and dance halls. And over them all hangs a great fear, a fear which multiplies the number of suicides and fills the asylums with wrecks. No one is sure what the next day may bring, and the world they know crowds them out and does not want them. "This is the way the world ends, not with a bang but a whimper." Or to quote the lines of the Down and Out: "We challenge life no more, no more, with our dead faith and our dead hope: We carry furled the fainting flags of a dead hope and a dead faith. Day sings no song, neither is there room for rest beside night in her sleeping; We've but a sigh for a song and a deep sigh for a drum beat."

If this be true, is it not imperative that we should restore the faith in man once more—a faith which is futile if it be not founded on the hope of God? Half measures are worse than useless, and the present trend of morals, which claims to be up to date, is nothing but a surrender to this despair in the supremacy of man's soul. All man's glories have been won by bestriding nature and difficulties, not in creeping under them. The desert and the jungle and the sea and the air, the secrets of nature, the recalcitrance of fellow men, the lust and pride within, they have been tamed and set to man's purposes, and those purposes are centred in a faith which knows that man is more than matter, that he is free with a limited freedom, and that all the best we can dream of in this life is but a prelude and

31

foretaste of immortal happiness with God and with those we have known and loved on earth. I have not time now to prove to you the existence of a spiritual soul, of free will and immortality. Fortunately the Dean of St. Paul's is showing you the reasonableness of a belief in immortality. As to the other truths, consider but for a moment the process of your own reasoning, the thoughts enshrined in some ancient manuscript, the author of which is long dead, while his ideas survive; ponder over your ability to be yourself, your own witness of your private life, how it is possible for you to judge the desires which are also yours, to behold nature and perhaps the multitudinous stars of the firmament and hold all this for a long while in the grasp of your mind. Do not such powers indicate a royalty in human nature which is independent of the material world? The body is subject to a temporal rhythm and slows down into decay, but conscience and knowledge move ever onward and up. How the spirit and body are interrelated cannot detain us now, but the fact that we can stand outside our own activities and judge and order them, remove, so to speak, by our own power the handcuffs which fetter, means that our home is where truth and justice and beauty reside in God.

The conviction of this resting on a truth which can be proved, if it were not already clear to noble minds, restores the sense of dignity and worth to each individual man, and with that belief comes courage and strong love. I said in the last talk that Christian morals had taken what was best from the wisdom of the Greek and Hebrew and Roman. The Greek at his highest believed in the sovereignty of mind and reason and its power to control. He loved balance and harmony, and he composed a moral philosophy based on this belief in man. The happiness and well-being of man defined for the Greeks the meaning of ultimate goodness, and evil was reckoned a frustration of this moral ideal. Their great thinkers worked out a scheme of the virtues and vices in accordance with this pattern, and they considered those who scorned their golden mean, their Parthenon of character building, to be uneducated barbarians. Two things were lacking in this ideal. They lacked that profound sense of moral obligation which Christianity introduced, and they were somewhat blind to the interior worth and dignity of man as a person. For them it was foolish to be vicious and fine to be virtuous, and we must turn to the Jews for a more developed sense of moral obligation. Good in the minds of the latter did not

33

consist in enlightened self-interest or acting in accordance with reason; the rule of goodness was written in the ten commandments, in the law which was imposed on them from Jahweh, and this law had to be followed because it set men on the path of divine holiness.

The world is God's and we too are dependent on Him and His will is the law of our life. "Thy justice is justice for ever; and thy law is truth. Thy testimonies are justice for ever; give me understanding and I shall live." That our happiness is God's will and that His commandments are the means to it recognised by us as duties, these are principles which combine the wisdom of the Greek and Jewish morals. They are amplified in the definition of St. Augustine, that "the eternal law is the divine reason or the will of God ordaining the preservation of the order of nature and prohibiting its infraction." From now on the somewhat external morality of the Greek and the law of the Jews are intensified by the knowledge that a 'tender felicitous providence' sees into the crypt of our soul. Morality becomes primarily interior, and it is the intention, the good will which counts because we are persons with a life hid in God and known through and through to Him. What we now take for granted arose from

34

this, our acceptance of personal rights, of individual liberty and the worth of conscience. Each individual becomes a world in himself, a kingdom more precious than all the beauty of the Universe put together, more lovely than the flowers of the field or Solomon arrayed in all his glory. There is no distinction between bondsman and free, between learned and ignorant, the healthy and the diseased. Each must be treated as a princeling of the family of God, and each has a life which soars beyond the jurisdiction of man or State to be judged by omniscient truth and love alone. Such is the dignity of man, the worth of personality. It brings with it great responsibilities. Each soul is a world apart, and like a Ming vase can suffer irreparable damage if it be not carefully tended. Hence the high ideal of education and the sacred rights of the individual in the State. But more than that. Each soul is unique and can never be repeated; each has a function and purpose which alone he can fulfil, and again in the immense solitude of the self there is only one absolute love which can satisfy it. So great an ideal demands uncompromising standards of conduct; poised between heaven and earth, the breaking of a single one of the laws of its life must bring it crashing down, and it is for this reason that

Christian morals are inexorable on the duty of sacrificing everything—pleasure, success, honour and friendship—before yielding to lust or deceit and untruth or injustice or pride; and it is for the same reason that God has written in our hearts a law revealed by conscience which is so strict that it seems at first a prohibition and a frustration of much that we desire to do. If the eye be evil the whole act is evil. We are never out of the presence of living Truth and Love, and we grow or die by its absolute standards. Let us look at ourselves in the light of these principles. Immediately it becomes clear to us that there is much that is lawless in us, and our first object must be to tidy up the mess within. The means to do this is that which is followed with every design, mechanical or natural. The parts must work to the service of the whole. In our body we cannot afford to have the lungs or stomach or blood or brain behaving independently of each other. In a city, if one section acts the drone or idles the whole suffers. So too with human nature. We are composed of numerous functions and instincts, and we can misuse them by eating or drinking too much or letting the urge of sex have full play. Sentiment can become sentimentality, courage rashness, self respect pride, and so on. Each power in us must join in the pursuit of the ideal which makes us truly human and great. It follows therefore immediately that what we call vice is from one aspect giving in to the pleasure of the impulses in us when they do not serve the high purpose demanded of us by our reason. This is irrational; it is taking the hand off the steering wheel; it means liberty hall instead of order; it is like the folly of a general who lets his troops do what they like. But it is also far more than this. An act of gluttony, a lie against truth, an assent to lust reveals the intention and decision of a person who judges himself by absolute standards made manifest in conscience; it is the desecration of that lovely and holy thing, personality; it is an offence against the Universe, and finally it is a sin against the Living Principle of all that is fair and wise and loving, God himself. So grave a sin and offence is this that, as the Christian knows, it needs the death of the Son of God on a cross to make it as though it had never been and restore the balance.

For the moment, however, let us be content to realise that evil consists in breaking the law which governs the wellbeing of human nature, the law which is manifested in conscience, and this is the rational ground for calling a number of acts and thoughts wrong which do not affect anyone but our-

selves directly. There are some who think in terms
only of a social wrong and claim the right to secret
sin. But we are not persons for nothing, and being
persons we have responsibilities towards ourselves.
We have first and foremost to aim at personal goodness, initially by self-discipline and secondly by
the proper use of our talents and faculties. Self-
indulgence and sloth are both evil; evil also are an
utter disregard for our health without reason and
the misuse of our instincts or desecration of them.
These are some of our duties, and we have also
rights, the right to our liberty unless we forfeit it
by injustice to our neighbours—and even then that
interior liberty which is exhibited in free choices
and the following of conscience remains. As our
body is part of ourselves and made immeasurably
superior to that of the animal by its conjunction
with the spirit, it too must be treated with respect
and cannot be handed over into a complete servitude
to another. It is the organ of the spirit, the earth
giving strength and scope to the roots of knowledge
and virtue, and as even the body without some
additional property is not enough for the temporal
sovereignty of the soul, man has a right to property.
I do not say to all the property which men in fact
acquire and claim, but it is quite a different thing

to say that a man has too much and that this excess is at the expense of others and to assume that a body of men or a State has the power belonging to it to give or take away what is the right of persons. The latter is false and relies on a view which lowers the standard of human nature. If this be forgotten and we rely on humanistic arguments or take short-sighted views of our human nature, then will return not the Saturnian kingdom, but barbarism and the degradation of human personality, and no compelling reason will appear why men and women should not be treated as superior animals and be judged solely by their relative efficiency in the commonwealth; why the bond of marriage should not yield to an ideal of stock breeding. In fine there will be no safeguard for the weak and nothing but hollow sentiment against cannibalism. Between these two destinies we have to choose, and there is no other alternative.

III

DUTIES TO SELF, FAMILY, STATE AND SOCIETY

Up to now I have been putting before you the general Christian position with regard to man and how he should behave. This has been necessary because it is impossible to divorce morals from belief and in particular from our belief about human nature. I have tried to show you that there is a philosophy solidly established in reason and taking full account of experience. This emphasises the personality and dignity of man and sets his actions and ideals in a perspective where God is his beginning and end, and happiness is to be found in this life by the conquering of self and in the next life in an immortal union with supreme love and beauty. I have contrasted with this ideal the present change, or as I should call it, decay of morals due to a pessimistic view of man and the consequent betrayal of what is noblest in him. Let me go on from here.

Without knowing it many of our present moralists are showing themselves bad losers. You have watched

bad losers at outdoor games or indoors at cards.
They begin to complain of their luck, to find fault
with the game and its rules and others, indeed with
everything except themselves. In some cases, alas!
they begin to be unscrupulous in order to get
success and the pleasure they want, and they take
advantage of doubtful rules and cheat. In the same
way owing to the kind of talk that is constantly
going on and our present miseries, we are being
tempted to cheat life and get what we want without
being prepared to lose or count the cost. We want
security and ease, and to get them we will disregard
any dull moral law which stands in the way; we
want money and we want love, so if after playing
our cards and committing ourselves to marriage or
some other serious contract we find we are losing
we go back on our promises and break our word
and try to cheat against the immutable rules of the
game of life. We may not realise the enormity of
what we are doing (though nature generally pays us
out and nations suffer their nemesis), because we
have forgotten that the rules are exactly fitted to
suit man, and all his happiness consists in keeping
them. Notice for instance that risk is part and parcel
of our human joy, and risk means that we are prepared to abide by failure just as much as by success.

Notice again that the very tang of life is hardship, the strenuous effort to be more than we are and to give to others what costs us much sacrifice. Yet the modern morals are founded on pleasure and security, and, be it remarked, such a view can lead to only greater unhappiness because any life worth living must challenge hardship and overcome it. According to our expectations is our joy or disappointment. This present generation has been fooled into thinking that our present troubles are transitory and due to the madness of past generations, that there should be no trials and that communism or some other panacea will bring about universal good will and ease. As a result we do not take the trials and risks inherent in our choices and our promises as fair and necessary; we magnify the difficulty and mesmerise our will power so as to be helpless before it. Because anæsthetics are now used for operations (which our ancestors, knowing there was no escape, bore with resignation), we look also for anæsthetics in moral difficulties, and as I say, we cheat life to obtain what we want.

Now we can never be persons in the full sense of the word if we accept this point of view. It is utterly different from the Christian one which sets such a high value on personality and human nature that it will not hear of this cheating on any account. It says you have a soul and character, tender at first, which must be strengthened, and there are only two ways of life, the broad way of self-indulgence which is so easy and so contemptible, and the narrow way, hard and at times lonely, which will hurt abominably at times and may call for utter heroism through illness or desertion or misunderstanding. This latter is alone worthy of the spirit of man and leaves him at the end lovely and like to the son of God. It is the kind of life we instinctively admire, when we meet it in our neighbour or read of it in history or biography or poetry or fiction; in Socrates who would not swerve one inch from conscience; in Agnes, who kept her purity inviolate amid brutish men; in Augustine, who drew his soul like a sword out of the scabbard of sin. Our excuses and rational-isations for breaking vows and superseding the old moral laws and commandments are rooted in dis-honour and ask for a peace at any price. What it is to our honour to do as fitting the dignity of human nature and our responsibilities as persons I must now make clear. I should begin by explaining a difference between what we are bound under pain of sin to do and what love may persuade us to do. We may give away all that we possess, but we are

43

not bound to do so; we may for some cause choose virginity in place of marriage, but marriage is an excellent thing; we have a right to defend ourselves and resist aggression, and we may also offer the other cheek. Because one course may be better it does not follow that the other is not fair and good. Indeed the better may at times be the enemy of the good, but to this I will return again in a later talk. For the moment I am concerned with the distinction between good and evil, and not the better and the good, and we want to know on what principles to choose what is right. Once we clear away the mist encompassing our ideas about the purpose and end of our human nature, and keep firmly in mind what it is to be a person, the criterion will become straightforward in its application. We can do nothing which perverts the high purpose for which we were born. Just as with any object of value, be it a jewel or plant or animal, there are agencies which can do it good or destroy it, just as with our own body there are laws of health and disease, so too with our human nature. But because human beings are so infinitely more valuable than any material thing we know, the prescriptions laid down by the Lord of life and recognised within us as our law must be observed with the utmost diligence and without exception. Even supposing that these pre-scriptions were not vital to our spiritual health, it would be unsafe to disregard them for any reason. To stop rowing on a placid lake is sensible, but to do so against a running stream will be folly, and we know only too well that the current within us is perpetually dragging us back and drawing us to slackness, indulgence and license. Once let go and we are swept away.

The first law therefore is to keep the prow of our soul undeviatingly straight and the mind master of the rabble which may be an ally or an enemy. Each member of that rabble of instincts and impulses, each part of us has a definite function, and it has to be laced up to the one genuine ideal. This gives us a second law, that all our instincts must be used in their proper way to subserve the main purpose of the self. This is no strange criterion, for we use it without thinking in our judgments of ourselves and others. All recognise that to use another human being just for our pleasures is wrong, and similarly we condemn gluttony and greed and sensuality and avarice and selfishness. The ground of our dis-approval is that gluttony means indulging an appetite beyond what is good for us and blotting out the reason to let the animal prevail; in sensuality we indulge in sexual pleasure independently of the purpose which the instinct serves; the avaricious give undue attention and regard to what is at best only a means to the royalty of the spirit, and selfishness means again that we exaggerate our own claims and fight against the higher interests of our soul which is drawn up by love to identify itself with what is immeasurably higher than itself. Such conduct is irrational; it is vicious and contrary to the nature of man; it makes a schism within our personality and brands it and makes us false stewards, disloyal in the sin, to the Love which draws all things to himself.

For the moment, however, let us concentrate on the fact that evil runs counter to our good and slashes the fair picture of the self to pieces. There are some who think that evil is at most a social wrong and would judge it by its consequences. But we are not persons for nothing, and as such we have responsibilities towards ourselves and can do what is intrinsically evil. Our first duty is to exercise that proper control of our senses and passions which leads to self-mastery and self-perfection. Such a use of our talents is good, and the abuse of them bad. We are bound to take a sufficient care of our health, to eat to live, to exercise our minds, to avoid slackness and mere pleasure seeking. The principle, I hope, is clear, and you can easily work out for yourselves the application of it to our various appetites and powers. These will be our duties, but, as I have said, as persons we have rights, the right to live, the right to liberty unless we forfeit it by social injustice, and even then a degree of privacy should be ours and the freedom of conscience. Furthermore as our body is part of ourselves and through interaction with the spirit immeasurably superior to that of animals, it must be treated with respect and cannot be made just the tool of another's will. All our knowledge comes to us through sense, and our character and personality are developed by the body and its needs, and as even the body is not sufficient of itself to allow scope for the growth of our powers and personality, a right to possess and call things and property our own is a natural right of man. Undoubtedly there may be an abuse of this, and dire necessity may require that the individual sacrifice what normally he may keep; but there is all the difference in the world between saying that a State may confiscate at its will what belongs to persons, and that it may call on us to sacrifice a right owing to an immediate necessity, such as a famine or war. The former principle is false and

47

treats persons as if they were things or no better than cows grazing in a field. All moral principles should conspire to maintain and exalt the dignity of human nature, and so a medical profession should set itself to look solely to the preservation of life and health, and the legal to assume innocence till the contrary be proved; and civilised communities, in order to keep alive in the minds of all the hidden excellence of man, must endow with symbolic glory what is insignificant in itself, and insist on manners and ritual.

Thus we see how a clear conception of human nature and its dignity is the best guide in morals, and we can easily extend the rights and duties of each individual to social morals seeing that society is a community of persons. Each and everyone must be treated as an end and not solely as means; their freedom must be respected. We must treat others as ourselves, protect their lives, see that they have opportunities for developing their personality, hold fast to our promises to them, speak the truth and safeguard their reputation from detraction or calumny. By nature man is a social being; he is born into a family and he gives and receives in a community or State. A new set of duties and rights springs into being with these new units, and we have to work out their respective claims. This I will do next time, concluding with a summary of what is special to Christian morals. All the moral ideas I have so far expounded have their roots in the Christian philosophy of life. Take it away and we descend into a darkness of despair. Man suffers from a *nostalgie de la boue*, and left to himself he goes first to the City of Vanity Fair and then makes his habitation with the beasts of the field. The love of God alone can keep man true to himself and turn his errant mind and passions to fine issues.

IV

THE CHRISTIAN STANDARD AND IDEAL

I⊤ is commonly thought now that the only kind of
wrong we can do is social wrong. That this is false
I have tried to show in the last talk, when speaking
of personality and personal responsibility. The
Christian morality has always laid great stress on the
motive and intention. "The things which proceed
out of the mouth come forth from the heart and
those things defile a man." I repeat this because the
other night I was arguing with some young men who
seemed to have no idea of this. They thought also
that if morality did not depend on some such
formula as the greatest good of the greatest number
it could not be rational and must depend on feeling.
I have argued that morality is reasonable because it
is founded on our nature. We are not a chance
assortment of atoms assembled higgledy-piggledy.
We are a work of consummate art not yet complete,
and the end determines what it is right or wrong
for us to do. We have the wonderful gift of manag-

ing ourselves not so as to do what we like with ourselves, but in accordance with the divine artist's or Maker's will. He is truth and beauty; he is incomparably beyond us, but in Augustine's words, "There is One within me who is more myself than myself". And so we say "Thy will be done", and in our interior thoughts and decisions are in His presence and responsible to Him.

This interior life which is the secret of our liberty and personality, makes us each a separate cosmos, a world far richer than the material universe, and it begets a great loneliness within till we find the divine lover who is closer than hands or feet. This part of us is beyond the reach of the State, but as we are also social beings bound up by nature in a bundle with others and affecting others and affected by them every moment of our lives to their good or detriment, this personal life of ours spreads out into a social and external life and creates many problems which we must now discuss.

Of all the social relations we have with others there are two which are unique and essential. Man can live without trades unions or banks or golf clubs or universities, valuable as some of these may be, but he cannot live without parents and family and some sort of community life. That is obvious, but the consequences are not always accepted as obvious, so I ask you to listen carefully to them. Remember first what I hope I have shown you, that goodness and moral right descend from their source, God, and we sin or act rightly according as we guide our nature to the perfect end lovingly chosen for it. Now as a means to that end the family and society are essential; they have therefore in them the moral authority of God, and the members of a family or State have moral duties towards them. Let us take the domestic type first. A family consists of father, mother, and children, and it is even more fundamental than civil society seeing that the existence of the human species depends finally and completely upon it. You cannot overrate, therefore, the importance of the family, and you may say, moreover, that the decisive mark of a Christian civilisation is the high respect paid to it. Around us we see the decline of the family; it is no longer the unit to be considered first in all legislation and social improvement. The individual has taken the place of the family with disastrous consequences in housing, wages and education. The State interferes without any qualms in the concerns of the family, and the necessary properties of the family, permanent marriage union, duties of parents towards children and children towards parents are losing all moral significance. The State growing ever more autocratic interferes more and more, and with an inhuman thoroughness sweeps the streets and sweeps the home and sweeps family affection and family ties away.

The State occupies an extraordinary position in modern life. In capitalistic societies it is denounced by the revolutionary, but the changes whether of Nazism or Communism are no improvement; they are as far from the ideal as the woman who posed as the goddess of reason in Notre Dame. Having denied the divine right which belongs to God we have transferred it to the State with sinister consequences. I do not mean to deny the State some authority, but the extent of it must be worked out by reason from what we know to be the nature of man. I said that society is necessary for man's welfare and rudimentary societies grow naturally into what is called the State. I say naturally, because the eighteenth-century theory of some social contract is artificial and against the facts. When men come together there must arise in time some organisation which exists to provide for the common good, for the community as a whole, and this is the definition of the State. Disputes have to be settled, rights and

E   53

duties in regard to property and promises and contracts decided and the welfare of the community promoted by laws against disturbers of the peace and defence measures against outside aggressors. Hence a true State will be occupied in providing all that is requisite for the social welfare of its members. For this some authority is required and this authority can claim obedience in so far as it works on the whole to the good of the individuals composing it, and this authority will be seen in legislative, judicial and executive acts. But since it is composed of persons it is always limited by the rights of persons, and as its aim is to develop that personality, it cannot on any account treat them as mere units subordinated in every way to itself. It cannot override the family, for instance; it can no more break the marriage bond than it can demand of an individual person that he should lie or commit injustice and rob an innocent man of his right to possess, or of his life or liberty.

For this reason the philosophy of Communism is incompatible with Christian morals. No one will deny that the best communists are stirred by motives which do them credit and that part of their aim is identical with that of Christianity. The love of the poor and the wish to better them is derived from the Christian belief in the infinite worth of each and every individual, but neither historically nor doctrinally does Communism show any Christian tendency. The theory is bound up with a complete negation of the spiritual worth of man. It denies that a person is more than a resultant of economic forces; it takes away from him all that is most precious, his inner life, his spiritual liberty, and it hands him over body and without soul to the dictatorship of a small group calling themselves the proletariat. I know that there are men and women who write and talk of Christian Communism, and that there are as many interpretations of the theory as there are weeds on a badly kept lawn, but not one of these rank theories has been able to stand criticism. They are suffused with sentimentalism, and if one wishes for an authentic account one must go to those who are out and out materialists, regard religion as dope and in practice call for the heads of those who oppose them politically. (In passing let me say that I will deal in my last talk with the question that Christ taught Communism and that religious orders have practised it.)

Now some of you may say, why signal out Communism in this way when there are other forms of government which are equally, if not more, obnoxious? At least Communism has the material welfare of the poor at heart. I do so because Communism and Christianity confront each other to-day as the two clear rivals, and the future, I think, lies with one or other of them. (I know, of course, which will win ultimately, for the Church of God has worn out many hammers.) Other prevalent views seem when examined to be either variations on the despotism of the State, and made contemptible by some absurd theory of race or breeding or else we are back in capitalism. The trouble with capitalism is that it is so difficult to define. Since the beginning of time men have competed in honourable and dishonourable rivalry, and reward and possessions have gone to the clever, the skilled, the audacious and the self-confident, and though you may call ambition the last infirmity, it is the infirmity of noble man, and our duty is to sublimate it, not destroy it. The ancient Christian moral proclaimed the motto, *noblesse oblige*; it held that position and honour were founded on the service given and the self-sacrifice practised. The guilds served mankind by providing it with the necessaries of life, the doctor pledged himself to ease pain and preserve health, the lawyer protected the innocent and upheld justice, the warrior gave himself to hardship and even death for the life of the community, and the statesman spent himself for the same purpose at home, and the head of Christendom was the servant of the servants of God. This ideal, thank God, still persists, but many another theory, materialistic and cruel, has crept in, and with the support of banks and stock exchanges and a new business code has produced the gross inequality of our present society and the inhuman conditions of the poor. It is not my part here to apportion the blame. The evil and the good of our present society are so closely interconnected that practical reform is exceedingly difficult.

What is true is that reform can come only by Christian morals, by following out the principles of personality, its rights and duties, and justice and charity. The danger is that the State having lost its Christian belief and without any clear-sighted principle may take the easy way, and in the name of comfort and uniformity interfere with the home and the liberty of the individual, and, instead of removing the conditions which cause the innocent to suffer, Herod-like remove the innocents for the sake of material efficiency.

Of the type of State which would best exemplify the Christian ideal I cannot speak, as it would take a new series of talks. I hope, however, that there are not lacking indications of the principles on which it must be built, and thank God much consideration is being given to the problem. Nor have I time to dwell on the problem of internationalism and the League of Nations. Perhaps in the next talk, in answering questions, there may be an occasion to say something on these matters and the morality of war.

There is one matter, however—and that the most important of all—which remains over, and it will be well to make a beginning of it now. It concerns the contribution which the Christian religion as a religion makes to morality. To understand this you must not confuse the Christian religion with that vague religiosity or sentimentalism which so often goes by its name, nor put humanity first and God second, and estimate the worth of religion by its service to morals; I mean the humanitarian morals with its creed of decency and philanthropy. The Christian religion is the worship of God in Christ, and Christians are members of that society which has Christ for its head and for its end union with Him in eternal glory. The society is a supernatural one subsisting by the grace of God, and therefore independent of and higher than any human society.

The Christian, however, who is sworn into this fellowship with God and betrothed to him in communion is not released from his duties to the State and his fellow men; nor does he normally turn his back on them. His religion must come first, but as he finds the material for virtue in everyday life, he comes to his daily duties and human cares with a new willingness and a new motive. He does not try to serve two masters, because God, the love which moves all, is the end of all social virtue as of his religion, and he shoulders his burden and takes up the cross of his fellow creatures with a new love because his Master, being lifted up, drew all things to Himself, and the disciple is not greater than his master.

Next time I will complete these remarks on the motives the Christian can bring to make his conduct perfect, and then answer the questions which have been asked or may still be asked.

V

ANSWERS TO DIFFICULTIES

THE influence of Christian belief on morals can be roughly, if inadequately, summed up in two virtues, humility and charity. The Greeks taught something of the splendour of man; they bequeathed to us a true picture of man controlling his nature and the world around him by his godlike reason, and so made possible a civilisation in which art and politics and philosophy could reign. I said, too, that Christianity deepened man's knowledge of himself and opened out the interior of his soul, thus displaying man's true dignity and the meaning of personality. But were this the whole story, then I might almost be inciting you to pride. To be master of oneself, to be unbending against temptation, to be royally independent is all very well, but first it seldom works, alas! and secondly it may become all too easily only another name for pride. There is only one way to prevent this, and it is given to us in Christianity. A soul that is reliant on itself is doomed. The world around is too much for it, and though it be greater than the world, it is dwarfed by the infinite possibilities of heroism and beauty which dawn before its mind. We are but tiny nurslings sustained in existence by the love of God. So great is he and so much better than what we are, that were it not that we belong to him utterly we should despair. Confronted by his power and providence and love, we grow sick of self-love and ashamed of what we are, and to glory in our childish successes seems so silly and ungenerous that pride can have no entry. Thus truth destroys pride, and shame at our shortcomings and a happy joy in God's redeeming love makes us humble. There is the virtue of humility; it comes from truth or full self-understanding founded on the knowledge of God.

Next there is charity. It is a form of love and a form superior to any found before the coming of Christ. Unbelievers may scoff because there is a mystery in it, but the mystery is a luminous one, and it can be summed up in the words in St. John, "that they all may be one, as Thou Father in me and I in Thee, that they also may be one in us . . . that the love wherewith Thou hast loved me may be in them and I in them." Here we have an identification first of the love of the Father and the Son, and then of the Father and us through and in Christ. I say "identification" because although human language here fails, it is the best word for something which is really happening, and as long as we remember that the identification does not destroy our personality but heightens it, we can use the word freely and truly and not metaphorically. . . . All the Christian secret is here and all the dogmas flow out of this, the Church, the Eucharist, the Communion of Saints, everything! It means this—that Christ who is God and man can live and love in each of us, and that therefore we and our acts have a divine quality and our love is a divine love. "What you do to the least of these, you do to Me." "Saul, Saul, why persecutest thou *Me!*" Our neighbour is not just Mr. X. Y. with his pleasant or repulsive characteristics; he is the beloved of God, and more, he is to be regarded as Christ himself. Just as I can in all humility through grace cry out with St. Paul, "I, no longer I, but Christ liveth in me," so in dealing with my neighbour I have to remember that the love wherewith the Father has loved Christ is in them and He in them. I knew of a small newspaper boy who because of his zeal was stabbed to death during a recent persecution of Christians, and while he was being bayoneted, he kept crying out, "Christ my king, He lives in me and I in Him." Now if only this

62

be true—and all things are possible with God—and, after all, some such wondrous divine union is hinted at in human marriage—then a new motive is added to life, and you have the reason why Francis of Assisi bowed the knee in reverence to beggars, and Peter Claver kissed the wounds of the black slaves, and why Christian saints have soared into a contemplation of love which lifted them entirely above the earth, and why the Eucharist is the central mystery of Christian belief, and lastly why numbers in every age have been drawn by divine love apart, and lived like the little Sisters of the Poor, shall we say, poor, unmarried, and sacrificing everything.

In the light of this, let me now answer some of the difficulties which have occurred to you. To one I have already suggested the answer. You ask how Christian morals are higher than other codes. Not only because they are founded on the best wisdom of the world and have been worked into the most complete system man has ever known, but also because they have at their root this mystery of love which God has revealed to us in Christ. And so at the beginning you hear St. Paul bursting into that supreme praise of love which you know so well, how all without love is but a tinkling cymbal, and in practice treats the runaway slave Onesimus as

63

free and one with him in Christ. Nor does this mean, to answer a question bordering on this, that there are two moralities in the Christian scheme, one for the laity and one for saints. The love laid down by Christ is a commandment for all Christians. We must love God first and our neighbour as ourselves, and as we are each a facet of Christ revealing down the ages his many-splendoured beauty, which was too superabundant to be limited to any time or place, be it Palestine or Athens or Rome, we must love our neighbour as Christ. But while all are held to this commandment, not all are called by the same means to fulfil it; there are Marthas and there are Maries. The work of the world has to be carried on, and some are called to marriage and responsible positions, while others are led out from the distractions of the world, and free from the embarrassment of money and the pleasure of doing what they please, are able to give themselves without impediment to the love of God. These do not regard property or marriage as wrong, but they surrender the good that is in them, because in the vocation which is theirs such things are in the way. All life is made up of some sacrifice. To be good at anything you must discipline yourself, and if you take up one occupation you must abandon others.

But this is not the whole answer to this question. It is undoubtedly true that Christian morals allow a man to possess and nevertheless they echo Christ's words about the rich, allow Christians to seek redress in the law courts and yet bid them turn the other cheek and in various other ways seem perhaps to be inconsistent. Well, first remember this: Christ does not take away what is right and good when he advocates what may be higher. (Non eripit mortalia qui regna dat cælestia.) To possess property is a right of a human person, and nothing can make it wrong as it stands; hence the counsel to do without it may be a call of love to do something still better. Notice first that it may not be better. To get rid of all you have when others are dependent on you might be quite wrong, and again if you are not strong enough to live without possessions you may be doing a foolish thing. You will turn into that dreadful type of religious fanatic who is completely without sense. You can hear him in Hyde Park, and I have had letters from him during these talks. What I say of possessions holds also on the question of war and pacifism. This is not at all an easy question to be settled, as some of those who write and talk on it seem to think. You can't take away the right of self-defence, and though modern war is both so hideous and so futile that it is hard to see how it can be justified, that still must leave intact the right of any people to die if they so wish, like the Macchabees, in preference to surrendering to a false and cruel foe. They think it better to die than to live "eyeless in Gaza at the mill with slaves." This question is indeed a difficult one, and I only touch on it because no question asked me has directly sought for an answer.

Is not Christianity essentially communistic, and are not religious orders communism in practice? No! Christianity is founded on personal relations, and the early Church was not communistic. It left individuals free. The punishment of Ananias and Sapphira, in the Acts, was due to their deceit in promising to give what they had and refusing to part with all according to their promise. The element of truth in the question is this—that human beings through love of God should so strive that they become indifferent to material possessions. In other words, the ideal which individual persons may reach is to live poor and humble and loving. But it would be a mad folly to impose this ideal. It must come from the individual, and he should take wise advice before he tries to put it into practice. There are enough mad houses already. Religious orders are composed of these who voluntarily have given up their goods. Many are refused admission because they are not suited. This fact and the further fact that the well-known temptation of monks, which is mentioned in all spiritual books, is a form of sloth, are a weighty testimony against communism.

A question which was bound to be asked, and has been, concerns persecution and intolerance. I think a man is intolerant when he will neither examine his own prejudices nor the views of people with whom he disagrees. It is not intolerance to be hard on what is evil, or what you are confident after examination is evil. The sentimentalists tell us that Christ was infinitely tolerant, but they misuse words and forget the Gospels. (Why will people take what they want out of the Gospels, for example, the Sermon on the Mount, and leave out the rest?) Christ could not tolerate the Pharisees nor Herod nor those who scandalised his little ones. He cursed the barren fig tree, and He drove the traffickers out of the Temple with a whip. The Church begins with St. Peter striking dead Ananias and Sapphira. The more we hold a thing precious, the less tolerant can we be of those who would mutilate it or teach others to ignore it, and if we hold the message of God to be really the one hope of mankind, how can we tolerate those who would, by ignoring it, blaspheme the love of God, and plunge mankind into irremediable misery? Suppose that a group of men had been responsible for all the pain and anguish and hate of the Great War, and that you and I had known this. Would you have tolerated them? And there are worse evils than the misery of the Great War. Active persecution is, indeed, another matter. One who tries to put it in its right perspective is sure to be suspect, so let me say just this. Persecutions abound now, and there are thousands of Christians who have been murdered or put in prison or had their fair works burnt to the ground, and all they hold dear filched from them. They have not fought back; they have borne it all with patience, and the remnants have gone into exile. Whatever be the past of Christianity, in this it still shows the thorn-crowned visage of its Master and is alive.

Many questions I must leave unanswered, but there is a group which can be taken together. They have this in common that they are pseudo-scientific. Have not scientific discoveries made it clear that many of the old moral beliefs are false? Has not medical investigation shown that character is dependent on psycho-physical conditions of the body, and has not psycho-analysis made clear that the

68

unconscious is more important than the conscious? A modern jury ought to consist of medical men and women. To those who think this I answer: all honour to those investigators who have added to the wealth of our knowledge, but I am sure they would be the last to say that they have cleared away the mystery of human behaviour or the influence of mind and will on health, and conduct. Of course, our character is affected by our body, and our will by our instincts and passions. Why, Aristotle knew that, and there is not the slightest reason for thinking that recent discoveries have disproved the old truths. All they have done is to make clearer the relation between our freedom and its conditions, and it remains as true to-day as yesterday that by force of an ideal the spirit of man can ascend to heights and animate his body to exertions and endurance which shock common sense. And as for the unconscious, as the whole object of psycho-analysis consists in bringing to consciousness what has been repressed, it is absurd to say that the latter has ceased to be the decisive factor.

I must now end. Many questions I have left unanswered, and I must plead time as my excuse. Some questions could not well be answered in public, and some which have been on religion could

F   69

not be answered without leaving my topic. Some letters have been mainly abuse, and I ask pardon if I have given cause for it.

One last word. There is an unchanging moral standard founded on wisdom and truth. Do not listen to the sophistries which advise a change of moral to suit new problems and modern times. Justice does not change nor charity, nor any of the fundamental truths and virtues. Judæa, Greece, Rome, France, Spain and England—these have grown at different times into great peoples, and they did so by the practice of the same virtues, and those which have fallen have fallen by the same weaknesses and vices. We cannot escape doom by calling vice virtue, and if we fall through weakness, we shall not rise up by saluting our fall as a new experience or liberation or new ascent. Again, we can never rise to moral grandeur without reliance on the living God. It is told of St. Thomas Aquinas that once Christ seemed to speak to him, and ask him what reward he wished for serving his Master well and faithfully—and St. Thomas answered: "Only Thyself, Lord." There love and loyalty join hands and the perfect moral is revealed.

PART II

ELUCIDATION

I

THE GREEK MORAL IDEAL AND
CONSCIENCE

In the broadcasts I have insisted on the undying value of the Greek conception of morals. The Greeks formulated an idea of man which has served ever since to distinguish civilisation from barbarism. The strange creature who hunted and fought, married and had children, made cities and laws, discovered in the maturity of Greek culture the formula which conditions human wellbeing. It consisted of a proportion and control, the control of reason which gave the right proportion to the undisciplined feelings, passions and desires. The city is the individual writ large, and just as in a city there must be a unified direction and the subordination of various functions to the chief end, so in the individual what is below reason must be governed by the reason to the proper welfare of the human being. As we all know, the idea of a mixture, which contained various elements mingled in their proper propor-

73

tions, permeated Greek art and philosophy. The serene balance of Greek statuary, the precise perfection of column and temple, the dislike of ''the loose, the lawless, the exaggerated, the insolent and the profane'', all proclaim the ideal at which the Greek aimed. Plato in the Philebus points the same moral when he says: ''The goddess of the limit, my dear Philebus, seeing insolence and all manner of wickedness breaking loose from all limit in point of gratification and gluttony and greed, established a law or order of limited being; and you say this restraint was the death of pleasure: I say it was the saving of it.''

The civilised man, then, is like one who makes out of a jungle an acre of well-cultivated land, and man alone of animals can do this, because he is a rational animal. The reason in him is not content with things as it finds them; it must introduce or discover order; it must measure and define, and it must set the whole of its own nature in tune with its proper perfection. Aristotle—and we can take Aristotle as the most representative of the Greek thinkers—begins his great work on morals with what to him and his contemporaries would have seemed obvious principles or platitudes. He says that every science and art aims at an end or good, and this end may lie in the activity itself, as in thought, or in some product, such as a boot or bridle. Applying this to action, we must seek for the end or good to be obtained, and amongst the goods there will be the ultimate good, desired for its own sake, and subordinate goods which lead on to the ultimate end and may, perhaps, constitute it in some sort. This introduction serves to define the nature of the study of morals, and the rest of the work of Aristotle is devoted to the analysis and description of what is the good for man. His method is to find out by analogy from other things, artificial and natural, what is the function and purpose of human nature. We know what a good shoe is and how to make one. What then is the function of man, and how can we make good men? If we can find what makes a man to be a man and not, for example, a horse or dog, what differentiates him from all else, we shall be hot on the scent of our quarry. Now there is one thing which is peculiar to man among the beasts, and that is the presence of reason; hence the perfection of man will lie in the proper development of this reason in relation to the animal in him and in its own right. From his other works Aristotle takes over a division of the parts or characteristics of human beings. There is a part which is not subject to reason, that is to say, the life processes which are common to all living things. Another part is not rational itself but can listen to reason; it does not originate rules, it accepts them. This part consists of the feelings and lower desires, and the feelings are those, particularly of pleasure and pain, which arise according as an object is felt as helpful or harmful. Lastly there is the activity of reason itself.

Nothing need be said about the first part. The second deserves a long treatment, and Aristotle tries to show by means of his celebrated doctrine of the mean how the feelings promote the welfare of man. It should be remarked that this doctrine applies strictly to man considered only as a psycho-physical being, as he omits for the time all consideration of the aims of the highest parts in man and their consequent effect upon our behaviour. To explain more clearly what is meant by this, let us take the word "health" and the example of a man in search of it. For bodily health he will consult his doctor, and from him he will learn how best to keep his body, that is the part of him which is irrational, in a good state. He will find something analogous to Aristotle's mean even here. If he tests his weight on a modern weighing machine he will see set out the proportions which normally ought to exist between height, age and weight, and again he will learn, if he be in training, that there is a right amount of food to be eaten in accordance with the exercise he has taken and the present vigour of his body. This proportion will differ with every individual, but for each one there is a proportion or mean which alone is right. Let the man now consult the health of his character. He knows that he is too easily upset or too impatient or irritable, too cowardly or too foolhardy, too apt to toady or be rude to those in a superior position. "Was I too excited and fierce? Did I meet the occasion properly? Was my behaviour just right?" These and similar questions show that the words "too much" and "too little" are applicable also to our feelings and actions, and so Aristotle holds that it is the task of reason to exercise that moderation between excess and defect of feeling and that the result is moral virtue. In acting bravely we curb the natural impulse to run away; by temperance we give the bodily appetites their due enjoyment, whereas when we leave the feelings and passions unchecked we fall straightway into vice.

The activity of the third part of the soul is seen in science, art, prudence and wisdom, and it is this part which fixes the far-off end which is the co-ordinating principle and standard for all the activities of human nature. If we accept the theory of Jaeger, Aristotle, as his life advanced, drew further and further away from Plato and thought less and less of the spiritual kingdom whither Plato held all our ideals should be directed. As more representative than Aristotle of this spiritual tendency among the Greeks I may quote the following from Plato: "The kind of madness which is imputed to him who, when he sees the beauty of earth, is transported with the recollection of the true beauty; he would like to fly away, but he cannot; he is like a bird fluttering and looking upward and careless of the world below; and he is therefore thought to be mad. And I have shown this of all inspirations to be the noblest and the highest, and the offspring of the highest in him who has or shares in it, and that he who loves the beautiful is called a lover because he partakes of it. For, as has already been said, every soul of man has in the way of nature beheld true being; this was the condition of her passing into the form of man." On the nature of this ideal Aristotle has something to say, and in the Ethics he tells us "to play the immortal as far as we can". But undoubtedly his work on Ethics suffers for lack of a clear end and clear perspective; he prepares us for a vision of ultimate truth and seems to vacillate between a purely temporal and humanitarian ideal and a vague making ourselves like to the gods. For this reason he has been harshly judged, and it is common to find modern English moralists condemning him because he has sketched a view of pleasure or happiness which leaves out the essential of morality, namely, duty or consciousness of moral obligation. Even M. Gilson has no high opinion of the depth of his moral views. He writes: "We should look in vain for any such conception (i.e. divine commandments and the sin of breaking them) in Aristotle's moral doctrine. Attentive to all that conditions morality, he classifies with minute care the various errors that go to vitiate our acts, but his analysis never takes him higher than the human reason. At the basis of all his analyses and all his conclusions lies Socrates' fundamental principle: all wickedness is ignorance. . . . Aristotle, in fact, regards man as engaged in the pursuit of a happiness —for the rest a purely relative happiness—the achievement of which is the term of the moral life. Actions are good in so far as they tend towards the goal, bad in so far as they tend away from it; in any event his conception of moral good or evil is closely allied with the idea of success and failure." And again: "Virtue is the rational habit that puts us in

79

the way of attaining happiness, just as vice is the irrational habit which condemns us to miss it. In all this there is no hint of any law higher than that of the human being, we get the benefit of our address and suffer the consequences of our awkwardness; absorbed in the contemplation of his own thought, the First Unmoved Mover makes no attempt to legislate for man. . . ."

This is not the place to discuss fully the justice or injustice of this criticism, especially as in the text I accept the importance of the Hebrew concept of divine law and its influence in filling up what was wanting to the Greeks. As the same time it is easy to be unfair to Aristotle and forget his aim. The aim of his ethics was to give a complete text book for legislators in order that they might bring up the youth of their cities in the right way. While, therefore, it is true that Aristotle leaves out all mention of God and consequently fails to provide a full explanation of moral obligation, his analysis, so far as it goes, can be defended. We cannot argue that we feel morally obliged to do a certain act because we know that God commanded it. To say this would imply that we had no sense of obligation until we knew that there was a God and that He wills us to do this particular action. The action is not right merely because God told us to do it. God being goodness itself ordains the act because it is in accordance with his goodness. Our goodness is founded on God's, and therefore we instinctively, so to speak, have an aversion from certain acts and an inclination to others. The full explanation of this instructive reaction to good and evil is only revealed after careful thought, and the sense of moral obligation will persist, even when this true explanation is doubted or denied. Where pagans and agnostics are likely to err is in their inability to see that certain definite kinds of actions and thoughts are wrong. They lose gradually that delicacy of apprehension which is conspicuous in the saints, and some alas! begin to take as justifiable injustice in business and personal impurity and talk of "hard cases" and take as the standard of their conduct temporal happiness.

We all begin, therefore, with a rudimentary idea of moral obligation. Were this not so, the fact that God is our beginning and end, and the Lord of justice would not evoke any moral response in us. The meaning of duty must already be fixed to some extent in our minds, and the explanation for this Aristotle half provides. He gives us as a formula "what is in accordance with right reason". These words have puzzled commentators, and most prefer to use in their translation from the Greek another word than "reason" for "logos". This latter word does indeed cover many different shades of meaning, and it can be used, for instance, to express thinking as opposed to perceiving or imagining or the process of reasoning as opposed to intuition and sense experience, or again as the faculty of mind as opposed to emotion and passion. Most of us use the word "reason" to include more than one defined sense, as when we ask a man to "use his reason". When Aristotle invented his formula of living according to reason (logos) I think he had something in mind which most of us, if not his commentators, can understand. Every natural object around us has a definite nature, and according to that nature does it act and react. By means of these actions and reactions to tests in laboratories scientists make and confirm their discoveries. There will, then, be a rule or law by which objects are governed, and so we speak of birds flying, fish swimming, carnivores eating flesh, acorns growing into oak trees, and caterpillars into butterflies by a law of their nature. The law is what each thing must do because it is determined to do so by the kind of nature it has. Human beings are like to other things in having a nature, and this nature will lie heavy on them and act as a law predisposing them to certain actions. But there is this peculiarity in man, which, as Aristotle declares, separates him from all other living things. He is endowed with reason, and reason means first that his own predispositions will be apparent to him consciously or as an idea in his mind, and that secondly this predisposition will normally, and when he is not carried away by violence within or without, move him as an inclination or desire. In his mind he will see not what he must do but what he ought to do. By the law of its nature the moth rushes to the light and may destroy itself in the flame; by the law of his nature man recognises a strong inclination to what seems to be his good, but he can distinguish between what will burn him and what will illuminate him. To act according to reason means therefore that man follows what his nature as mirrored in his reason demands of him, and this is to live by the highest faculty he has and to direct himself to what is his good.

If after this explanation it still remains obscure what part duty and conscience play in the Greek account of morality, we can disperse this obscurity with the help of the Hebrew notion of the Commandments. To the Jews life consisted in the relation of human ends to divine purposes. God is the author of human life and has ordained what is to man's welfare and the divine glory. Human beings are all subject to the one true God, and the Jews are his chosen people, who keep the Commandments and the law given to Moses from on high. In this conception we see how duty and conscience are intimately connected with knowledge of a God who is the sovereign Lord. The external commandment of God is also the rule of reason, a reason, of course, enlightened and directed.

It is possible, as the lives of many of our fellow countrymen prove, to accept a sense of duty without realising it to be also a law of God; and there is a school of philosophers which concentrates entirely on this sense of duty and denies that it has any connection with a divine will. It goes so far even as to dissociate duty from goodness and perfection, and argues that duty cannot be derived from any idea we have of our good. This latter view is strongly maintained in certain learned circles, but it is so paradoxical that it will never make a popular appeal, and for that reason I will not dwell on it here. Suffice it to say that it makes the most of a difficulty in the Greek view of morals at which I have already hinted. The Greek, when he chooses to be good, is acting in accordance with reason. All his actions should be eminently reasonable, and Socrates suggested that evil is in the last analysis always error. Each individual, when confronted with a choice, must act on reason, and when he has weighed conflicting desires of what is to his good, it can only be an error of judgment if he decides to follow what is evil. Evil by definition is what is bad for his human nature; it will destroy him as surely as the flame will destroy the moth or arsenic the life of our body. Now there are at least two mistakes here which should be noticed. The first is that the explanation does not really provide a complete account of conscience, and secondly it does not tell us why we may not, if we like, ruin ourselves. To take this second point first. I may be unreasonable in choosing to tell a lie or cheat my neighbour. Let us grant that this is evident, though, in fact, it does not always appear to be so. But is my conscience nothing more than this feeling of being unreasonable? If this were true I who am master of my nature could choose to act unreasonably with it. I would be foolish, but not immoral. For my action to be immoral I must not merely be going against what I recognise to be my own best interests and defying reason, but offending against a law which is not of my own making. This law imposes itself upon me first as an "ought" of obligation to which I am subject, and secondly as a rational obligation which is as fixed as truth. Implicitly, therefore, in the immediate awareness of this obligation there is present the idea of a cosmic, absolute realm of which I am part, and once a clear conception of the world and of God is presented, as in the Jewish religion, I can see explicitly that duty and moral obligation spring from the relation between a creature and his maker. The point to notice is that in relation to man God ordinarily acts from within him and not from outside, and the reason for this is that man is a rational being and with his own mind has to act for himself and think for himself. With the great exception of the Christian Revelation, which is concerned with what man could not discover for himself, man grows by effort to a knowledge of himself and nature. God does not put knowledge ready-made into his head, or call him from without, as he did Samuel. Similarly man comes to desire what is good and to realise the reasonableness and duty of pursuing it. The command of God is played within in the key of man's nature. The Creator makes Himself felt not by thunder from above, but in the still small voice, not as a voice coming from without, but in and through the rational nature which He made. As the reflection of a face in a mirror or still water is really the same face, as what we think of things is really the things themselves as well as our thought of them, so our conscience is the rational dictate of our nature and also the command of God.

But it may be said, "Does not our conscience err? And is it not dependent on some special sense or emotion?" Our conscience does certainly err, and precisely for the reason that it is the command of God translated into the idiom and terms of our own nature. If we are the stuff of which cowards and brutes are made our conscience will be clogged by that and show what we are; whereas if we are of the stuff of which heroes and saints are made we will have a pure mind and sensitive conscience. All of us grow in delicacy of apperception if our education has any formative value, and the more we habituate ourselves to the good life by action the keener does our moral judgment become. Those who are like to God recognise His voice and know His word. And it is this fact which explains in what sense conscience is affected by emotion and temperament. Conscience is called by the Greeks the practical judgment, and in this definition they found the truth, but expressed it narrowly and too exclusively. It is we who judge, and our minds are seldom a pure ray of thought. We bring to our opinions and judgments all the bias and weight of our character, and so our conscience is drugged or pricked by what we are. Moreover, in practical judgment as contrasted with scientific judgment, another co-efficient is bound to enter in. Practical judgment is of action and of ends to be gained, and we cannot act unless we are moved in some sort by desire. The whole machinery of the human person is motionless until interest starts the wheels which revolve until finally the body is set going. Now desire can be sensible, as in hunger or concupiscence, or spiritual as in social reform or marriage friendship. These two may and do conflict and both have to be judged by reason, as both can be erratic and disordered. A drunkard is pulled too strongly one way, and a communist desires the material security of others to the exclusion of their personal and spiritual interests. In many of our choices we may not seem to be troubled by conscience. In choosing a Christmas present for a friend we select within our means what will please them. We may gamble at cards for small sums and be carefree in mind. But if we were to risk others' money or bet beyond our means when others are dependent on us, or with the knowledge that we were indulging a vicious weakness in our characters, we should be doing wrong, and conscience would be active. This implies that conscience is active in practical judgment whenever our spiritual or personal good is at stake, or in other words that our nature, like our own body, protests at its misuse and signifies in its own way what is to its good. And as this nature bears on it the perpetual imprint of the divine will which made it and conserves it, conscience, unless misdirected by our habits and education, can be called the law of God.

II

MORAL JUDGMENT

In the broadcasts I may seem to have assumed that
moral judgments are based on reason and that
conscience is no mysterious kind of sense or faculty,
but a particular kind of moral judgment. There have
been many theories of conscience, and it is usual
to-day to hear that morals and feelings go together.
They do indeed go together, but not in the way
which is supposed. Morals are essentially connected
with desire, and desires may be irrational or rational.
The task of a human being is to make his desires
reasonable, to stand above the crowd of them and,
despite their shouting and booing and urgency, to
persuade them to a course which is worthy of the
high purposes of a man. A man, whatever the
extreme school of psychologists may say, is not just
a jungle of different and competing animal passions
and instincts. He can recognise within him a law
which tells him what is good for him and for others,
and it is reasonable for him to make order within

himself and subordinate his powers to one supreme task. This supreme task which, because of its magnitude and distance is at first vague and unappetising, is described by the word, morality, and what we mean by morals is the acting in accordance with what we ought to be. An animal simply grows by the innate force within it, which is the co-ordinated system called its nature, into being a good or bad specimen of its kind. A man also grows bodily and spiritually, and as he has a mind he is able to superintend that growth and to judge it by standards which belong to the order of truth and absolute goodness. With the help of these standards we gradually work out what is good and what is evil and put selfishness, cowardice, meanness, dissipation, bestiality and pride on one side and honesty and sincerity and courage and forbearance and generosity on the other. These distinctions are not based on feeling; they exist, and we understand them because they bear on the perfection of man.

In normal circumstances the judgments of reason and the feelings go hand in hand. When one watches an act of cruelty one knows that it is unworthy of man and unfair to the victim, and a feeling of indignation is aroused at the sight. Hence as a short cut the feeling is often taken as a sufficient evidence of the presence of evil, and in an ideal society the feelings, being perfectly trained, would tell us the truth. Unfortunately the feelings, being a very fickle and capricious body, are always attaching themselves to false causes and confused cries, and so they have to be checked by reason. A good example of the error to which feeling is prone is provided by sex. It is a fact of experience that certain young people, when they are told the facts of sex, react with violent feelings of repulsion, and if their feelings made up their conscience they would be forced to regard all that has to do with human intercourse as wrong. Fortunately reason can come to the rescue and point out that man is made up of body as well as spirit and that the body so far from degrading us can be used to the noblest ends. The conviction of this can correct the bias of the feelings and so form an enlightened conscience.

At the back of the ready judgments which we all pass at every moment of the day there should lie some great rational belief. It is the duty of parents and of a Government to see that children are brought up in some such high belief, at first in the practice of it and later in the loving understanding of it. Fixed and orientated to what is noble, the whole self grows harmoniously and its spontaneous judgments will be backed by truth. Unfortunately in the England of the nineteenth century the intellectual background of the habits and practices which ruled everyday life was forgotten or repudiated. As a result convictions passed into conventions and these were imposed as rules of good conduct, as if they had come down from Mount Sinai. The feeling remained as an aftermath, like the brief light which remains after the sun has set. To-day many are impatient of conventions and feelings, for which no justification is offered, and for some reason best known to themselves editors of newspapers appeal to cinema stars and young sportsmen to give their opinions on fundamental questions of morals which have exercised the greatest minds from the Greek civilisation onwards. At the moment the leading thinkers in our two oldest Universities debate end-lessly whether duty is independent of goodness, and if so, which comes first, and our dramatists and essayists tell us that morals must be made to fit the economic and materialistic pressure of the times, and our novelists claim that everything should be experienced. No one dares to ask what is man that we should be mindful of him, and, fixing some standard guided by his ultimate end and perfection, inquires what is expected of him and what are his rights and duties. Until this is done conscience must be as uncertain as any weathercock, and the old unappeasable premonitions of right and wrong will be applied spasmodically and haltingly by individuals to the conduct of others but seldom to themselves.

No proper analysis or explanation of moral judgment and conscience is possible without taking into account the nature of man, and if it be said that this is to explain the obscure by what is still more obscure, the answer is that what is given to us immediately in conscience helps us to know what we are and what we are helps us to understand conscience better. This is not mysterious. We all of us have some idea of ourselves, but that idea can be made much more clear and profound by experience and by examining our activities, and in the same way conscience tells us our immediate duties and is like a signal telling us which way to proceed. But as it is concerned directly only with a present duty and is stupid or enlightened often about that, it has to be taught, and at the same time co-ordinated with what we know about our nature. To put this in another way, conscience is a department of the self, with its own proper business to perform, but it will help to the better running of that business if the nature of the firm is understood. In distinction from the animal kingdom we human beings have been given a mind and will to enable us to take an active part in the making of ourselves; we cannot make ourselves as we would like, and it needs great attention and sincerity not to trick ourselves and fail. We are aided in this by the natural set of the mind to truth and by a natural movement within us in revulsion to what is bad. Just as the physical appetite rebels against what is detrimental to the health, so the spiritual appetite in us rejects what is against its good, and this latter provokes the judgment of conscience. We know, however, that the instinctive taste and distaste are rudimentary and can be deceived, and that is why above I called the rudimentary sense of right and wrong a premonition. Like fear, it has the useful function of safeguarding our interests, and the wiser we grow the more does it turn into a practical judgment based on our knowledge of ourselves, our neighbour and God, and informing us where our perfection lies.

To some fortunate souls conscience and a sense of God are inseparable. To St. Augustine, for example, and to Newman, conscience meant much more than it means to us. The majority of us realise moral obligation only as a dead imperative or duty, and we do not pass immediately from the murmur of our nature to the author and maker of its commandments. We are too thick-skinned, but for St. Augustine and Newman the quickening sense of the commandment told them of Him in whom we have our life and being, and they shared the privilege of the mystics who pass their days in a hidden dialogue. How intimately our judgments of right reason and the voice of God in conscience are connected I have already explained in the preceding appendix.

A life then which will be fitted to our nature and a life which achieves this and more by submission to the law of truth and goodness imposed by God and known to us by conscience, these two complementary notions are found in the well-known definition of St. Augustine: "The eternal law is the divine reason or the will of God ordaining the safeguarding of the order of nature and prohibiting its infraction." The law, be it noticed, is no mere external one, but expressed in the unconscious order of physical and animal nature, and in us consciously through our knowledge of ourselves in conscience. As we have seen, duty and rights and authority in the home and in the State issue from this initial idea. Good conduct and good behaviour in the State are now no longer external acts; it is not merely that man makes a mess of his life by evil; he damages something which was meant to be of immortal beauty and he offends against a living source of justice and love.

I said that the pagan moral did not take sufficient notice of what we mean by person. We now think in terms of person and liberty and rights and private conscience. These are the gifts of Christian morality. The Gospel made it clear that the old distinctions of slave and citizen of a State were inapplicable, for we were citizens of no mean city and all free as the sons of God. And so from an external ethic of conduct the emphasis changed to a law of interior holiness. Each man is unique, an edition de luxe, and his worth is beyond all price. The true meaning of Psyche has been found, and the true meaning of Eros. The spirit of each of us is an ode of praise far more beautiful than the vast panorama of the Universe with its ranks of stars and flowers of the field arrayed in more beauty than Solomon. The abyss of the soul in its solitude can contain within itself this world and a thousand others and not be satisfied; it is a sounding-board which can give back in its own individual way all the minor themes of nature and life, and it is moved by a law within to call out one beloved name, could it but happily find it, a name murmured within the soul, and one to which all other names of love call and point. Law therefore without, love within, the spirit of man dark to itself at the beginning and ignorant of all that is outside searches for happiness and meets an order of nature and truth which it must obey and an interior voice which checks and commands. This harsh mystery of life is resolved in the Christian philosophy which shows that conscience is but the shadow "of love outstretched caressingly", and that by the force of truth and unchanging moral laws we are being lifted up into our own bliss and the enjoyment of eternal love. Thus the pagan cult of happiness or virtue for virtue's sake or duty which makes such dry bones comes alive. It is in the Christian scheme that man, as St. Augustine says, "goes forward with a sure and steady step in the best and happiest life. For what we chiefly wish to know in moral matters is what is man's sovereign good, that good to which all else in life is subordinated, and beyond this there is little else to be sought. We have shown by reason as far as we are able, and by divine authority that enlightens our reason, that this sovereign good is none other than God himself.

For what could possibly be better for man than to cleave to what really makes him blessed? Now this is God alone to whom we cleave in no other way than by affection, love and charity.''

It is natural in such a view that great stress should be laid on interior holiness, and from the earliest times we find Christian moralists insisting on the importance of intention. The intention formed and chosen makes the human being innocent or guilty before God no matter whether the act be carried out or not. ''If the eye be evil the whole act is evil.'' God knows our secret thoughts, and the things which proceed out of the mouth come forth from the heart, and those things defile a man. We are never out of the presence of Living Justice and Love, and Truth hates the lie in the soul. The more this interior disposition is emphasised the more does the sacred personality of man stand out. It is not exterior action or organisation, not legal persons like the State, which are ultimately good and evil; it is the soul fixed in a resolve, the interior choice and the orientation, and all things, success, material happiness, riches, honour, comfort and fame, fade into insignificance before the rectitude of the spirit of man, his resistance to temptation, his unswerving loyalty to those laws of the eternal order of God written in his heart. The effect of this attitude is seen in our legislation, our customs, our manners, our promises, our loyalties. We are taught to respect the conscience of other people, we must give them their privacy and what helps their personality, that is, the right to own themselves, their liberty, their body and their possessions. We swear fidelity to another, and so great is the interior sovereignty of this act that it must remain firm against all the onslaughts of time. To be forsworn is to blaspheme against the high status and purposes of man. Again in our education we must foster this interior liberty, this interior realm of the spirit, and in our relations with one another we must live by justice and courtesy and reverence. We cannot interfere with the logical and gracious structure of Christian morals without bringing the whole house of morals down upon our heads, and we ought to watch with the greatest suspicion this tinkering at moral laws which is going on nowadays in the name of happiness and abominate every theory propounded to us which belittles man and his soul and his freedom and his vocation to the most splendid and the most arduous of ideals. These latter theories catch us on our weakest side by an appeal to our sentimentality and our desire for immediate cures. They feed us with sweetmeats and sap our interior strength; they offer us vainly the whole world and suffer us to lose our soul.

III

THE SPIRITUAL PRINCIPLE IN MAN

THE main questions of morals are insoluble without some knowledge of the being who has to be moral. Hence it will be useful to summarise here some of the arguments implied in the text which go to prove that man is a spiritual being and endowed with free will.

A. *The Spirit of Man.* If we analyse what we mean by civilisation or culture we must admit that it means at least this, a growing appreciation of the things of the spirit and the subjection of all else to spiritual standards. Man ceases to behave like a beast; he controls himself and sets his mind and will to control nature. So it is that we find a code of morals taking shape in every civilisation, and with it an interest in the arts and an attempt to know nature and use it for human purposes. The degree of culture reached by any people will be measured by its moral ideals, its artistic achievements, its science and its religion. I will add, also, its humour.

On all these counts human beings manifest themselves as incurably spiritual. To take humour first; it is a gift which seems to belong exclusively to man. Animals have high spirits and can play, but humour relies on an intellectual insight and escapes them. In nursery rhyme and not in fact the "little dog laughed to see the sport". He cannot do so because humour depends essentially on some contrast between the lordly pretensions of man and his ridiculous plight, between the magnificent Guardsman and the street arab, Don Quixote and his "noble" steed Rosinante and Sancho Panza. Great comedy is like to great tragedy; they both see man capable of high heaven and tumbling to the pit of Hell, and that is why we laugh at man one moment and weep the next. Humour therefore witnesses to the existence in man of something dual, and it needs a mind to discern the contrast between these two infinities.

So too with art. No animal stops to admire the sun setting over Richmond Park. It is moved by beauty on occasions, and when we examine these we find that it is inseparably connected with instinct and purpose, when, for example, mating time draws near. There is no evidence that beauty is loved for its own sake, and consequently animals have no art, and pass by a picture of Botticelli's or Greco's without a flicker of interest. And if God gives them beauty, though they toil not neither do they spin, it is that beings with a mind may have enjoyment of it, and from such vestiges come to a knowledge of what beauty in itself must be. Once more, then, the existence of a spiritual principle is suggested, and this is confirmed by the power of knowing which is ours. This gift makes a gulf between man and all else below him, and the likenesses which strike the eye are superficial compared with this vast difference. The knowledge which animals have of us appears to be only a phosphorescence of their desires and passions; whereas we have a science of them, as we have a science of everything material, and so potent is our mind that some have thought it to be the creator of the pageantry of the world and the sole genuine being. We admire the grandeur of the Universe and we forget that without mind it falls back into uninterpreted movement, the movement of blobs of matter or vain radiation. We cannot indeed think of the world around us apart from its laws and patterns of behaviour; it is our science of nature, even more than nature itself, which is so impressive, and this fact is sufficient to show the pre-eminence of mind over all matter and the unique position of man in the world.

Whether we consider the results of mind or its activity the conclusion must be the same. Animals have been trained to feats of remarkable "intelligence", but even the most surprising, such as those of Köhler's chimpanzees, lack what is characteristic of man. This latter can be described either as the power to think abstractedly or as the power to know things as they are in themselves. The human mind is able to abstract what is general from particular instances and apply it to other examples. Given the example of a triangle or syllogism the boy or girl can on future occasions, despite all the differing kinds of triangles and syllogisms to be encountered, recognise a common universal quality which is absolute and true and apply it with certainty. Furthermore the mind can reflect upon this abstract idea and independently of its settings analyse still more clearly its meaning and deduce certain other ideas from it. The philosopher constantly does this, and the scientist is checked until he clarifies the ideas he is using. This general idea lifted out of its material husk is responsible for man's progress, and leads to the use of language—for what is language but the attempt to fix and use these ideas by means of sounds and symbols?

It is strange how so many blind themselves to this

manifest prerogative of man. There are some who try to reduce all our knowledge to sensible experience, which they say we share with the animals. But consider what happens to any human being in the short span of a day. A myriad influences play upon him and are transmitted, so it is said, to the brain, and there they are located and telephone wires connect them up and perhaps a replica for memory is prepared. But this is a travesty of experience, for we suffer millions and millions of influences each day, and they are all different, one from the other. So far as the sensible appearances of colours and sounds and shapes is concerned there is never an identical repetition, and this holds true even of the patterns we see, such as words, boxes, pencils, foods and clothes and faces. No Eastern djinn could sort out such confusion, and it is quite impossible that the brain bursting with goods piled up in its chambers should pick out tiny identities where there is no mark given to enable it to do so. To call a thing by its proper name we need to summon a power which can recognise meaning, and meanings which belong to things while they are constantly changing. Like a good librarian this power does not put books into shelves according to the time order they are brought along, nor does it arrange them by shape or colour, but fixes them in their proper places according to title and subject. In the welter of experience the mind distinguishes what is the meaning of things, and abstracts that meaning and is interested in it for its own sake.

Below the activity of thinking there are many other selective agencies, and with the help of these animals can also distinguish one thing from another in experience. But the selection is always pragmatic, the intelligence always being at the service and acting in the interests of the living body. In man the mind is disinterested, though this unselfishness also proves to be the making and perfection of human beings, and freed from servile tasks this mind is able to act in its own right and see things as they are. This is to step from darkness into light, from catacombs to Paradise, and if we but ponder over this privilege, we shall see that it gives the open sesame to all the glories of man. The mind sees things as they are; it is disinterested and therefore knows other things as other things, other persons as other persons. This means that the whole world is opened to us and that being or reality becomes in a sense ours, and if reality, then also truth. All living things grow by taking in substance from outside and converting it into their own being; the mind, too, which grows, and is far more alive than a material organism, takes in and makes its own all that falls within its capacity. But as we have seen, the mind feeds on all reality, and like a bee extracts its honey, but without harming a particle of that reality, and yet so as to leave nothing unsipped. I can know the secrets of the fields and of the hills, know my friends and know and love them for what they are. The wise man has within him all the wealth of the world, and a lover is one with his beloved. This and much more comes from our having a mind, but I must limit myself to pointing out the conclusions to be drawn about the self and its spirituality. A mind which can be everything as well as being itself, and indeed be more itself by being all things, is of a completely different pattern from that of physical things, which are essentially exclusive the one of the other and live by separateness and destruction. According to theories of evolution there must be a struggle to survive, species must live on species, but minds do not struggle or collide; they communicate and share. Physical things, too, are always changing and have their rhythms of growth and decay; the mind grows, and wisdom has no end, and goodness ever climbs. The law which governs advance in moral perfection and science in each individual is the opposite from the advance of his bodily vigour. The best athletes have to retire after the age of twenty-five or thirty, as already the limit of their physical perfection has been reached. But their spiritual advance is still near its beginning. It has an enemy of its own kind, in the frustration or perversion of error and sin, but these do not destroy. The soul is not doomed by time, and the mind never ceases except when the physical instruments which safeguard memory and the senses fail, and even then we can witness the spectacle of a soaring and generous mind overcoming the decrepitude of old age and illness.

There is in man the subject or principle or soul which is fed with truth, grows in perfection, while the body decays, to a grandeur which is fixed by standards of absolute goodness and beauty, and tries to confer immortality on all it touches. It is altogether another life from that of the animal, and it is proved to be such by its ability to stand off from itself and lead a kind of double life. We are so accustomed to ourselves that we do not realise how strange, and indeed impossible, on any physical explanation, is our twin act which makes us both to be doing something and at the same time the spectator of our action, to be subject and object, to be and to know our being partially, to be servant and judge of ourselves at one and the same moment. The explanation is the presence of mind which makes us know ourselves as we are and serves to constitute us as persons. We think of personality as something private, sacred and incommunicative. An unconscious being might be a substance, that is, a being which is dependent on itself, as a dog has its own life and is not part of anything else, but it cannot say, "I am myself". Mind makes the difference, for mind makes the self conscious of itself to itself, makes it conscious of standards to which it must conform, standards of truth, justice and love, and gives it responsibility as having the power to know what is to its good and to follow that good. Even a baby can be called a person, not as having at the moment consciousness and charge of itself, but as having the principle within it whence these powers are derived. Each human being, then, is a separate cosmos able to reproduce within in a unique way all the splendours of the universe, and express them in terms of its own love, and this makes every person unique. Again, because each person has for his end something infinite and perfect, he must be regarded as sacred and above all other values. On no account can he be sacrificed for any lesser good whatsoever,

and it were better that the whole world should
perish rather than that the spiritual part of him should
be lost by compromise with evil. Lastly a person is
lovable without end because he is created in God's
image and he possesses in miniature something of
the undying splendour of God.

The divine commandments and the Christian
code are supposed by many to impose an intolerable
yoke upon man, thwarting his freedom and crushing
his individuality. They can be hard and they do involve at times sacrifices which to the unregenerate
must seem futile. Draw the curtain over man's
personality and end, and this is inevitable. We are
dying to-day for want of dogma, for the soul of man
unless it be fed on truth wanders restlessly in dry
places. All human beings form for themselves, consciously or unconsciously, a vision of peace. Taught
nowadays from early years to distrust all the deep
wisdom stored and exhibited by Christianity, we
expect instead to find a rapid happiness increasing
from the time we come to the use of reason. This
expectation is the mother of unhappiness, as our
disappointments are always in proportion to our
expectations. We do not complain because night
follows the day, and the reason is that we know it
must and should do so. Our ancestors did not com-

plain because they lacked the advantages of hot water and central heating, for the reason that they did not expect such luxuries as normal. Most of us now would be unhappy without them. This law, however, assumes gigantic importance when it affects our attitude to life. If girls are brought up to esteem motherhood and regard it as both a duty and a privilege, the pangs and the prospect of many children do not fret the mind. But if on the contrary a generation is taught from early childhood that personal happiness is its due and that all that involves pain should be avoided or remedied, a distress and even a neurosis will be caused by the prospect of many children. This example can serve as an illustration of the general point of view which is prevalent, a point of view which is humanitarian and can be gentle and kind, but is radically based on a disbelief in any destiny of man save that of general prosperity in this life. At its worst it spells a peace at any price, whereas life and Christianity are continually hammering in a lesson of peace at a very high price. Life at every turn gives the lie to the gospel of easy prosperity. No amount of hygiene will remove illness and the decay of senses and members of the body and the chance of accident, and no social planning can remove the necessity of servile work and a division of it into grades; and we have not yet found any resource against the vices of envy and jealousy and hate and selfishness and self-indulgence.

The humanitarian ideal which puts second things first cannot succeed against the adversities of nature, physical and human, and it degrades man. To pitch his ideal low is to take away from him what he most enjoys, namely, victory over difficulties. The higher a type of being the greater must be the care taken of it, the more arduous must be its task and the greater its fall. One can never swim any distance so long as one keeps one foot on the bottom, and it is impossible to have the adventure of flying the Atlantic by sliding on a shallow pond. God gave us an ideal which ought to make us proud, the while it frightens us by its height. It is a challenge to us and a compliment, and it confers an exalted dignity on human nature. All our morals must be worked out in relation to this ideal, and Kant had a glimpse of the truth, when he gave his impractical formula for action that we should generalise it and see whether it would become every man and in every circumstance. Such a law would save us from playing with evil and making our personal distress and difficulty an excuse for indulgence. We kick against the goad and call it cruel, and do not realise that in removing it we have taken away a stimulus to perfection not only from ourselves but from all others.

It is on these principles, beginning with the spiritual personality, on the power and duty of maintaining the self and advancing it by struggle, and on the consequent dignity of our nature, that we must work out our duties in regard to ourselves and our neighbours, and set a high and inflexible standard for self-discipline, justice and charity. It will be found that nearly all the innovations in morality which are saluted as progressive are really denials in some form or other of the dignity of man. Divorce made easy, sterilisation, euthanasia, companionate marriage and birth control, some forms of pacifism, social tyrannies and Communism, they all bid adieu to what is the vital spring of man's welfare and let the enemy into his soul by making him content with what is less than the best.

B. *Free Will*. Strange to say at a time when liberty is on everyone's lips, it is openly taught and commonly believed that there is no such thing as free will. This is but one example of the inconsistencies of modern life and the growing schism in man's soul. We have a bundle of likes and dislikes but no steady all-embracing outlook. Philosophers have decided that it is wisdom to wear blinkers and moralists are content with pleasure as a standard. When Bertrand Russell writes that man's "thoughts and his bodily movements follow the same laws that describe the motions of stars and atoms", he is denying freedom as well as talking nonsense, and yet for him freedom is indispensable for the happiness he craves and preaches.

The simple practise freedom and esteem it in others and in themselves, but when asked they often deny it because they have been told in early youth that there is no such thing, or because they have read in the papers that some scientist has disproved it. The learned deny it because it is no longer fashionable, and think that it is an antiquated and clerical superstition. Throw it out however as often as they like, it will always return, for we cannot do without it, and all our lives, all our judgments and estimates depend upon it. Like equally obvious truths, such as the difference between matter and mind, love, death and immortality, it is in our system, and we would die were it taken away. What then does it mean? Not some mysterious faculty which gives us omnipotence, nor some *deus ex machina* which enables us to act in an arbitrary manner and entirely out of keeping with our habits and character. There are some who propose a dilemma and fancy that it settles the question. It runs as follows: either the will acts with reason or without reason; if without reason then free will is irresponsible and irrational, if with reason, then the strongest motive or the character must determine the choice. The fallacy here lies in supposing that the defenders of free will ever imagined that the will could act without a motive. The point of freedom is that of two possible courses the will is inclined with desire or motive to both. Hence whichever is chosen the act will be motived and reasonable. But does not this imply that the strongest motive must prevail? The second fallacy consists in asserting that there is such a factor as the strongest motive. It begs the question. If the strongest motive prevailed we ought to be conscious of it, feel, so to speak, the door closing despite all our efforts to hold it open, experience the cock motive conquering all the others. But nothing like this happens normally. There are occasions, of course, when we are swept away by passion or overcome by inertia, when we cannot get out of bed in the morning or behave like Tristram after the love potion. We may, and probably do, often fail to gauge the pressure on us of habits, and think we can throw them off whenever we feel inclined to do so. We forget that without some stirring attraction or ideal we shall never be the heroes we pretend to ourselves we can be. All this is true, but when we have before us a definite simple choice to be made we are conscious not of a strongest or stronger motive, but of the fact that neither is so strong as to prevail on us unless we make it the stronger. It is just because we are inclined in two ways and that the inclinations are incompatible and both desirable and possible that we have perforce to make one of them our own and be responsible for it. How fortunate it would be occasionally if we could in conscience say that the inclination was too much for us and that we did not deliberately betray a friend or shirk a duty. We are only too anxious to make excuses to ourselves for guilt, and the very fact that we try to persuade ourselves that we did not realise what we were doing, that it was an accident, that we were obsessed or forced or out of our wits or unduly influenced, shows clearly that we distinguish clearly between acts when the strongest motive prevailed and when we ourselves made a desire into a resolution for which we are responsible because free.

The basis of free will is again the dignity of human

nature. We are not like the lower animals determined by the instincts of our nature to a certain
type of action. The soul of animals is in their vital
activity, but in man it rises above its own activities
and can look before and after. It is both what it is
and what it may be, and what it may be is there in
prospect and in the form of an idea in the mind.
Hence the soul in its mental activity is detached
from the body and can gaze upon and judge itself.
It is not in servitude to the needs of its individual
nature; it is rather a citizen of the world and all
reality. A world of beauty and goodness unfolds itself before the mind and gradually takes shape in
an infinite number of loves. A human being can be
in love with anything because he is in love despite
himself with the end and consummation of all loveli-
ness, God. Being content with nothing but the best
he is not determined to this or that and he can never
be constrained by the magnetism of any object he
beholds. It satisfies him in part, but it always has a
rival. We all of us have a number of interests, and
there is no proportion between the liveliness of
these interests and their value as recognised ab-
stractly by the mind. We know that the discovery
of a manuscript in Samarkand is more important
than the result of a local soccer match, but we get

the evening paper to find out about the latter not the former. Duty, which is nature's admonition of our true welfare, is seldom supported by sensuous desire, and the fact that there can be such conflict within us only goes to prove the obvious truth that we are not perfect at the beginning and have to strive to orchestrate our various longings into one true love. Until we are perfect we shall always be capable of choosing badly and making the worst appear the better, and our act will be wilful and free.

What I have written so far will, I hope, serve to show that the usual attacks on free will rest on a misunderstanding. Of the old difficulty that freedom is impossible because of the uniformity of nature, I need say nothing. That difficulty was a bogy of Victorian science. It is now held that science does not deal with causality at all, that nature and the scientific descriptions of it are only distantly related, and there are even some scientists who are prepared to deny any determinism in the material world. These conclusions may be as ephemeral as others recorded in the nineteenth century; what is permanently true is that the modern scientific method deliberately limits itself to a certain way of approaching nature. It omits, but does not deny, what concerns us as human beings most of all, the world, that is, of quality, life and value. The Marxist is also committed to determinism, the determinism of economic forces, but, as I shall have something to say on this view later I can leave it aside now. The modern psychologists are shy of free will, either because they have no theory of the self, or because they believe in unconscious determinism. The nine-teenth-century psychologists gave up belief in a sub-stantial self, and their science has suffered ever since. Successions of sensations, streams of consciousness were the first substitutes, and as these failed to explain how the hero on the stage and off stage could be the same character, they invented an unconscious instead of returning to the old and sane view of self and person. So far as free will is concerned these psychologists are unbelievers. They hold that the unconscious, not the conscious, explains our conduct, and conse-quently we are in sooth determined by unknown factors, and our conscious decisions do not tell us the real story. That there is something here worth investigating no one will deny, and we are far too aware of self-deception and perplexities in our con-duct to rule out hidden causes. But it should be noticed that these hidden causes only limit the width of our freedom; they do not destroy it. We are all of us quite aware that human freedom is limited by human ability, and that there are innumerable things we cannot do. Each individual is faced with the problem of his powers and their extent; he knows that early upbringing has formed his likes and dislikes, that country, locality and perhaps inheritance and food have given him the material on which he has to build that perfection which will be his and his alone. These facts make up the problem of each individual's freedom; they do not destroy it. And if what the psychologists tell us is true and suppressed memories, or whatever we like to call them, press upon us in unsuspected ways, this new impediment must be added to those we already recognise, and that is all. But usually it is not the fact of an impediment which is new, but the source of it and the explanation. A man suffers from irresistible fears in certain situations; he is well aware that the fear robs him of his freedom; what he did not know is that this fear is due to an early shock and that it can be cured. Of course, if the psychologist goes on to say that all life is dominated by certain instincts and that what we call reasonable judgment is nothing but a rationalisation, then indeed freedom is cut away at its root. Such a view, however, is no more than a hypothesis and is not borne out by facts.

The difficulties, therefore, which have been raised against free will are not so serious as they have been supposed to be. The same human mind which suffers from infirmities discovers the objection and answers it, and the same mind which is captive to the unconscious is responsible for all that is known about the unconscious, and cures itself of its own weakness. It is preposterous to put the mind under a tombstone and then ask it to write its own obituary notice, and it is disastrous to bury freedom and personality these days and not to praise them. For a beggarly theory of the unconscious which is full of holes and tatters we give up the one living and glorious view of man.

I have sketched the nature of our freedom and must leave a number of interesting questions which arise in the attempt to analyse it into its components. Such an analysis demands a treatise by itself. There are the facts which prove our free will, the fact that we are conscious that in judgment we do the choosing and are not forced by anything but our own act to do what we are doing. We are conscious of *why* we are acting as we do, and if the value of this evidence be denied, then all evidence from consciousness must be thrown into the dustheap, and included in that evidence would be all certainty, everything in fact that has ever been said against free will. There are the confirming facts that we know quite well what checks our freedom and the compulsion exercised by weakness or passion. Our moral life has no meaning if we are not responsible for our actions, and if the stimulus to personal effort be altogether removed. Of the nature of our freedom I have given a hint in the analysis of our divided self and our divided loves. Given a reason which marks us off from all that is material and animal, we are able to superintend the movements of our nature, and with the guiding stars of absolute truth and goodness guide ourselves to our unique destiny.

This brings us back to the fundamental notion of the dignity of human nature, and the high warfare which is the life of the soul. This is the cardinal point of moral philosophy and all social and personal "welfare-planning" should lay stress upon it.

IV

BIRTH CONTROL

THE advocates of Birth Control claim both that it is a necessity and a proper means to bring about a social change for the better. When Malthus first drew the attention of the English people to the need of control he was not so much inspired by some high ideal as frightened by the prospect of a world in which the population would increase so rapidly that the earth would be unable to provide enough to feed them. He argued that over-population was the cause of poverty, that the population increased by geometrical progression, whereas food products increased only by arithmetical progression. Hence a grave danger lurked in the future. No one of his arguments is sound, as I hope to show, and he himself did not advocate artificial birth control. He turned, however, men's minds to the problem, and gradually other issues became intermingled with the first problem. The industrial system lowered the standard of living, and as a result the health of the nation suffered. The rapid advance of science led to its application in matters of health, and so a new ideal was evolved. This ideal may be called eugenic, and its method is to use all the resources of science to produce a nation of able-bodied, intelligent human beings. There is clearly nothing wrong with such an ideal, though it may easily turn into a sinister policy, and it too often relies on a very unidealistic conception of human nature.

I should like you to be under no misunderstanding of the Catholic position on this point. It is sometimes criticised as being anti-social, as discouraging birth control of any kind. Such a criticism is far from the truth—but it does disagree profoundly with the philosophy and practice of many who are birth-controllers and eugenists. In this view, man is a moral being with duties and rights—and the ideal is that he should be free and use his personal freedom rightly. When then it discovers as it thinks that the eugenic theory treats man as little more than a superior animal, and interests itself chiefly in producing a capable animal by means of medical science, it protests against this insult to human nature. Furthermore, it suspects the motives of those who speak and write contemptuously of the poor and of the unfit. Those who are well-off and blessed with the means both to nourish children and give them a suitable environment, ought to be especially careful in suggesting remedies for those less well placed. If evils attend the circumstances of the latter, then the cure should be to change these circumstances and not to legislate as though their condition were a permanent and acceptable law of nature. As Mr. Chesterton once remarked, if there are ten small boys who need top hats and there are only eight top hats, the proper plan is not to cut off the heads of two of the boys, but to make two more hats. This solution is all the more necessary, if the other alternative be a crime, and according to the Catholic practice, the remedy of artificial birth control is criminal because immoral .

Let us then see on what grounds artificial birth control is said to be immoral. I say "artificial" because there is much confusion owing to the use of the word "control". Control in this matter need not be sinful, in fact it might become a duty and certainly is praiseworthy. A man and a woman marry, and marriage is a holy contract whose end is the begetting and education of children, mutual support and affection and a remedy for lust. It is therefore an act with a moral end, and, furthermore, as both parties are human beings, it is fitting that the bodily enjoyment should serve the higher aims of the spirit. To bring out what I mean, I may recall a conversation with a young and ardent Socialist in a train between Cambridge and Bletchley. He told me with some fierceness that if he ever married he would be guided not merely by strong physical attraction but by friendship and nobility of character. I have never met him again, but he had seized hold of a vital distinction. The pleasure of sexual intercourse is shared with us by the brutes, and that pleasure in a moral being must be co-ordinated and sublimated by the end of marriage. In the human contract, then, the end of marriage dictates what is right, and lest the aims and feelings aroused grow too strong, a certain degree of continence is requisite. The degree of continence will vary with different parties according to their knowledge of themselves, of their strength and weakness; it should also be governed by the opportunities of fostering and educating the children of the marriage. That is to say, sexual intercourse is lawful and good in itself, and its use should be governed by the mutual consent of the parties as moral beings. Nevertheless since they are moral beings they have to consider their own dignity as human persons, and keep uxoriousness away and anything degrading, and they ought also to consider the future and the needs their children will have. This means control by continence or abstention, and this is the proper means of control because it means self-control and no interference with the right end of the marriage act. Clearly, however, it is difficult to lay down any laws in this matter. A husband and wife may decide that to safeguard mutual happiness they can risk the future, for after all the future is very uncertain, and there is no certainty that a large number of children are less likely to survive or lack sustenance.

The point of all this is that free persons marry and have therefore a perfect right to the marriage act and its pleasures provided they carry out that act so that its proper end be not frustrated. If the fruit of that end be one they cannot afford, then in their moral capacity as free persons they may practise continence or come together when there is less likelihood of generation. On this philosophy man is left free to determine himself, and he is excited to virtue. The opposite theory does not appeal to personality and freedom; it would remove the need of continence and self-control and provide a means to enjoy the pleasure of an act without its responsibilities; it secures the future by freeing the married from solicitude, and in doing so it approves, in the eyes of Catholics, of the end justifying a bad means.

The sin of artificial birth control is known technically as Onanism, from Onan the son of Her, who as the Book of Genesis narrated, did a deed, for which "the Lord slew him because he did a detestable thing". Onanism then may be said to cover all acts which in the sexual intercourse positively prevent conception. There is no specific difference whether one follows the method of Onan himself or uses the devices which have now become well known. The only difference is that modern methods are easier, and less physiologically harmful. Throughout the history of Christianity it has been viewed with special abhorrence as a grave sin of impurity.

The rational grounds for its condemnation have been already suggested. The voice of conscience— and by conscience I mean our practical reason—has declared as strongly against it as against fornication and adultery. The argument is that a function of nature must not be perverted to other ends and that pleasure in defiance of the proper functioning cannot be chosen as a good. As might be shown at greater length in moral philosophy, the object sought by the will must be good, and success in the attainment of that good is accompanied normally by pleasure. The hungry man seeks for food, and food satisfies the appetite. Any human appetite or activity in so far as it is natural can be satisfied in a proper way, and there is no evil in enjoying the pleasure if the pleasure be the resultant of the proper functioning of that appetite. Thus it is permissible to enjoy a good meal, to exercise one's limbs, to study, to enjoy the rights of married life. But always must the pleasure issue from and be subordinate to the end of the appetite or activity. The Roman vomitorium was therefore a perverse practice, and rightly disgusts us, the habit of lying likewise repels us because it is against the primary end of speech; drunkenness, embezzlement of funds by a financial agent, corruption in a cabinet minister, all fall into the same category. They are perverse—and that very word brings out the nature of the evil. Now artificial birth control means nothing else than that we pervert the use of the marriage act, and herein is the intrinsic evil of the practice; the end is thus frustrated and pleasure tends to be made the end. Even when those who practise it claim that they are acting for the social good of the State or in the interest of the children they already have, they are making an end justify a radically evil means, while those who are impatient of a restriction on their pleasure are pleading for the doctrine of the vomitorium and sacrificing duty to indulgence.

It is not then surprising that tradition has classed this practice with those sins of impurity which run against the laws of nature described by St. Paul as debasing the coinage. Ethically the sins of unnatural vice are even less excusable than prostitution and adultery. So conscious of this have been civilised communities that the right use of sexual intercourse has been safeguarded by laws which may be said to follow from the natural law. Sexual intercourse may be practised only after a matrimonial contract, which should be indissoluble, and the reason for this is that we all instinctively realise that the end of such intercourse is the perpetuation of the race, and that children cannot be brought forth and reared save in a family where the relations are permanent. Strict and immutable laws are absolutely requisite in this matter, because, however much eugenists try to hide the fact, it is notorious that mankind is barely able to hold its passions in check. The sexual is the strongest of all instincts, and requires therefore all the combined efforts of law and highmindedness to keep it from destroying the higher life of the individual as of the community. To open then such a broad way for the gratification of one's impulses as that of artificial birth control is to court disaster. To admit that indulgence in this matter may be an end in itself, is logically to weaken the arguments against other perversions and promiscuity. If the use of contraceptive methods by married people be not wrong in itself, then every married couple may decide so to act when they please, always, if they like; and again it is much harder to defend the indissolubility and exclusive rights of matrimony. As the consideration of children may be left out of account with the use of safe contraceptives, and as sexual pleasure independent of its main purpose may now be regarded as a legitimate end, it is difficult to see how such intercourse can logically be denied to the unmarried. The needs of the child and of the family are the warrant for a permanent contract, and with their disappearance, we are left with a right to polygamy.

It is well known that the publicity given to birth control has already had alarming results, and the wholesale practise of it by unmarried girls and boys brings us near to the evils which destroy a nation. Logically, as has been said, this result may be said to follow from the abandonment of a fundamental moral principle. But apart from logic, it is not in human nature to practise continence when illicit

intercourse is made so easy. Once allow that pleasure may be taken independently of duty, then with
the pressure of the sexual urge so strong, the laws
and sanctions of civilised life are sure to crumble.
Historians must have observed that the severance of
duty and pleasure is a symptom of decline in a
nation. Duty becomes irksome and is evaded, and
science is invoked in order to escape the nemesis of
this evasion. Self-control gives place to mechanical
control, and pleasure is substituted for the moral
ideal. A policy therefore which legalises pleasure to
avert certain evils is penny the wise and pound
foolish. Like Ethelred it buys off the Dane with gold
and only increases the burden and danger of the
future.

Such then is the moral argument against contraceptive methods or artificial birth-control. Without
doubt some of its advocates are stirred by high
motives. There are evils they wish to suppress, and
they see in birth control the means to suppress them.
The argument so far put forward against their
proposals is that they have chosen a bad means for
a good end.

I would now carry the argument into their own
country and suggest that birth control is not an
efficacious means to cure the evil they fear. In the

K   133

first place there are several unproved assumptions in the Neo-Malthusian theory. It is not certain that overpopulation is a cause of poverty, in fact evidence seems to show that this statement is false. It leaves out other causes and relies on the abstract proof that population outruns the food supply because the former increases by geometrical and the latter by arithmetical proportions. Now it is untrue that the resources of nature have been tapped and are not equal to the rapid increase of population. It has been said, for instance, that if England were as well cultivated as Flanders it would be almost self-sufficing. I will quote other pieces of evidence which bear upon this point and show how rash it is to dogmatize about population. "In the Suez Canal Zone there was a high death-rate chiefly owing to fever. According to Malthus it would have been a great mistake to lower this death-rate because if social conditions were improved, the population would rapidly increase and exceed the resources of the country. Now in fact social conditions were improved, the death-rate was lowered . . . but . . . the birth-rate fell too and the population remained stationary." Statistics from Japan show a similar story, and the only conclusion to draw is that the question of population is far more complicated than the Neo-Malthusians would have us suppose. There are many factors which have to be taken into account, and there is always an element of uncertainty. The geometrical progression is a myth, and so too is the supposed connection between a high birth-rate and a high death-rate. In French Canada, for instance, and in Connaught, where there is great poverty, there is a high birth-rate, and yet the death-rate in these provinces is lower than in Bradford, where there are maternity centres and every attention is paid to mothers and children.

It would appear that we can leave Nature to look after the question of population, and that there are laws which regulate births. Dr. Greenwood has given us a very informative census of 477 families. Of these 289 or 60 per cent limited their families and 188 or 40 per cent did not practise limitation. Of these 289, 183 limited their families by continence and 106 by artificial means. Nevertheless there was no appreciable difference between the two groups in the numbers of their children. Generalising, we can say that where humans may have to struggle for existence, there the number of births seems to be large, but when conditions are advantageous, then the numbers decrease. If this is so, then the fear of overpopulation is false, or rather the problem takes on quite a different complexion. It is poverty and evil conditions which lead to the evils eugenists are striving to check. They are horrified by what they call the growing number of the unfit. What then is their cure? If the generalisations I have made be true, their methods are a perversion of justice. They would legislate for the poor, treat them as a caste apart, and abuse their misfortunes. The only just procedure is to remove the evil conditions, not to interfere with births but to improve the environment.

As has been pointed out, the neo-Malthusians seek to spread the use of contraceptives because they see the ill effects and misery arising from large families bred in the deplorable conditions of one, two or three-room tenements in the slum quarters of cities. They should rather give their energies to the improvement of housing, the building of garden cities, the more equal distribution of wealth, the getting rid of smoke-pollution of the atmosphere, the perfection of locomotion between dwellings and places of work or business and in the education of children in open-air life and farm pursuits.

There is a great danger too of snobbery and ignorant reliance on science in the talk about the unfit. Medical science is still without any sure knowledge about inheritance, the relation of mind to body, the connexion between genius and madness. When Sir Isaac Newton was born he was so tiny that he could be put into a quart mug, and there are many instances of genius and intelligence which contradict facile assumptions about degeneracy and imbecility. Unfortunately a materialistic philosophy may easily take the reins in social legislation, and it would be the greatest misfortune if the ideal of free persons with souls were forgotten in the interests of breeding good citizens.

Lastly, it is important to remember that the medical profession is by no means wholehearted in its support of artificial birth-control. Books have been published by eminent doctors and psychologists which deplore the practice. They declare that it is not always a successful method—conception is not always prevented nor venereal disease. Again there is evidence that it has harmful effects on those who practise it. It tends to lead to sterility, so that married persons who leave the opportunity of children to the future find themselves childless when they want a child. Dame M'Elroy states that it has a bad effect on the nervous system, leading to neurosis and fibroid tumour, and she is supported in her opinion by the gynæcologist, Dr. Giles, and others. Furthermore, it is often the cause of unhappiness in marriage, and may have a bad effect on the child. A more serious indictment is pronounced by Dr. F. W. Taylor, who was President of the British Gynæcological Society in 1904. "Artificial prevention is an evil and a disgrace. The immorality of it, the degradation of succeeding generations by it, their domination or subjection by strangers—who are stronger because they have not given way to it—all need to be brought to the mind (of people). . . . It would be strange indeed if so unnatural a practice, one so destructive of the best life of the nation, should bring no danger or disease in its wake, and I am convinced after many years of observation that both sudden danger and chronic disease may be produced by the methods of prevention very generally employed." This verdict is supported by Sir John Robertson. Birth-prevention "leads to promiscuity and debauch and ruins the morals of those who use it".

If, then, what I have written in this paper is true, artificial birth-control is an evil in itself, which no argument can justify, and it is also, in the opinion of many experts, evil in its effects. In France, so M. Paul Burban tells us, the practice of abortion has increased *pari passu* with the use of contraceptives in recent years, and indeed it is difficult to see how morality which depends on a struggle against passion can survive, if the means for that passion are approved and legalised and put at everyone's disposal. As the *British Medical Journal* said in August 1921: "Morally the doctrine is indefensible; it follows the line of least resistance and sacrifices the spirit to the flesh. Naturally, it is fraught with grave danger to the home and to our national existence." Already social workers are growing alarmed at the spread of this vice amongst the quite young, and there is a question of appeal to Parliament on the matter; but whether young or old yield, it is the same vice of self-indulgence which has in the past destroyed inexorably both the individual and the nation.

r cf. Note B, p. 20.

r The *Church Times* for February 14th, 1930, quotes from an article written by Sir Leo Chiozza Money to the *Daily Herald*. The article gives the case against the sterilisation of the unfit and uses the results of an investigation of Dr. Lange, of Denmark. Dr. Lange investigated forty-four families, in which mental trouble had occurred. He found that, in addition to forty-four mental defectives, these families had produced bishops, cabinet ministers, statesmen, judges, physicians, university professors, members of parliament, schoolmasters, poets, painters, musicians and inventors, as well as a number of successful business men. The conclusion is that if marriage in these families had been prevented, Denmark would have suffered far more than it would have gained.

V

PACIFISM

THE Catholic attitude to war can be found admirably summarised in a booklet, called *A Primer of Peace and War*, which was produced under the editorship of the late Fr. Charles Plater during the Great War. I propose therefore to repeat some of the principles stated there, and then to discuss the momentous question of pacifism in the light of those principles and what has happened in the last twenty years.

War is the assertion of moral right by armed might. When there is a conflict of wills and every peaceable means of gaining one's right has failed—means such as appeals to reason, to conscience, to self-interest—then the only means left is that of material force. There must, therefore, be a moral right which has been violated and all other means must have been tried and failed before the last means of force can justly be applied. That the use of force on these conditions is morally right and at times obligatory everyone must admit. Those who doubt it are always presented with an extreme case, such as the defence of one's mother or of helpless children. If a man were carrying some antiseptic serum to a camp or hospital and on the use of it depended the lives of thousands of men, and an attempt were made to rob him of it, that man would have not only the right to defend himself but would be bound in conscience to do so by charity. Similarly a policeman would be morally bound to try, if needs be by force, to stop a white slave trafficker caught in the act or an American kidnapper of children. This moral doctrine bears also on the statesman who is responsible for the lives and welfare of those who have been entrusted to his care, and for that reason there can be no question theoretically of the right of a government to declare war when the conditions stated above have been fulfilled.

In more detail, we should distinguish war and civil strife, rebellion, guerilla warfare, punitive expeditions and private feuds. The latter can never be lawful in a civilised community, for the simple reason that justice can be sought and generally found in the law courts set up by the moral authority of the community. For the same reason punitive expeditions are justifiable only when they are led against a group of people who are not sufficiently

civilised to recognise any moral code whereby redress can be obtained. Guerilla warfare may be part
of self defence, but if there exist a government and
there be no authority drawn from it, such warfare
will usually be unjustified. Rebellion is justified if
the following three conditions are present, that the
Government has failed in its essential duty and the
people are in anarchy or under a tyranny, that the
constitutional means of redress have failed, and that
there is a reasonable hope of success. This latter
condition, which at first sight looks strange, is of
great importance, as will be seen later when the
question of pacifism is discussed. Civil strife is nowadays more likely to become rebellion and is
synonymous with revolutionary tactics.

War is like to these, but must be judged separ-
ately, and before we introduce the special problem
due to modern conditions, it is important to consider the issue in its simplest form, for otherwise
arguments for and against it tend to be very confused. A pacifist may have a righteous indignation
and choose the wrong argument to persuade others.
Let us now, however, introduce one of the compli-
cations of modern international relations, namely,
the difficulty of knowing what are the true causes
and motives of conflict. A just war must have as its

ground the violation of a right, of a right such as liberty of conscience, of person or of government, of national honour, the restoration of land wrongly seized, or the rehabilitation of justice violated on a large scale. For any of these reasons war can be called self-defence, and if there be a good accruing from it which is necessary for the welfare of the nation the physical injury and damage which arises directly out of war can and at times must be permitted. A small people like the Jews felt that their religion and national rights were so dishonoured that they rose under the Macchabees and were prepared to die rather than to submit to such iniquity. Here the cause and motive were noble, but in the last century, to take what is nearest to us, there have been wars fought to acquire more territory, to spread commerce, for dynastic reasons, to avert political disaster at home and to maintain the balance of Europe. Not one of these reasons is of itself moral.

Besides the origin and motive which determine the justice or injustice of war there is a third determinant, namely, the method. Methods of war have changed with the growth of civilisation. The end undertaken in war is by force of arms to compel an unjust aggressor to restore what is our due and

to make reparation. All that helps to this end might
be considered right, but in practice it is so easy to
use immoral means to this end and to let passions
control our actions, that civilised nations have
sought increasingly to repress all forms of savagery
and undue force. Even by the standards of pagan
and natural morality, massacres, looting, mutilation,
torture and reprisals against women and the innocent must be condemned, much more by the
standard of Christian charity, which is always com-
patible with justice. Though the dictum can be
wrested to hypocritical interpretations, it remains
true that in fighting or punishing one's enemy one
must love him. It is on this principle that in even
nominally Christian countries laws have been introduced to mitigate the horrors and sufferings entailed
by war, and there is no need here to give a list of
the Hague regulations and other rules which are
considered binding by civilised nations.

We are now in a position to consider the question
of pacifism. An extreme form of pacifism, which
condemns recourse to war as intrinsically evil, is
ruled out by what has been said above. If there be
a right belonging to human beings as responsible
persons, it cannot be that the maintenance of that
right is of its nature evil. What holds of the

individual holds also of a community of individuals, and just as I am not obliged to allow an aggressor to injure my property, myself, those dear to me or those dependent on me, so a community and especially those who have as their primary duty the protection and welfare of that community are not bound by any moral law to forsake what is necessary to their duty. Those who are more intelligent in their pacifism defend it generally on other grounds. They claim that as Christians they are bound by a higher law, or that war, as contrasted with private defensive measures, never attains its object, or that in modern conditions it is impossible to conduct a war which will secure its end or keep to moral methods. It is in such a presentation of it that a weighty case can be made out for pacifism, and there are responsible thinkers, Catholic and non-Catholic, on both sides.

These objections to war fall into two groups; the one concerns the method of war as a means to a good end in modern times, the second concerns the Christian attitude to it. The pacifist argument comes to this: we are bound to have a probability at least that in resorting to violent means a good end and one which has not a great proportionate evil attached to it can be attained. But in modern con-

ditions there is no such probability. Modern weapons of warfare make it a question of who can strike
the first blow, and by means of aeroplanes paralyse
a nation and inflict damage on countless thousands
of innocent persons. Of the nations which took part
in the Great War it is impossible now to tell which
was the victor and which the vanquished. Each
suffered irreparably, and in the economic inter-
dependence of modern states all are bound to suffer
the same disastrous fate. A new war would bring
with it inevitably the total collapse of civilisation.
Moreover, the evils accompanying any war now are
so widespread and horrible that they outweigh any
possible good to be obtained. Battles are not fought
between a few thousands of picked fighting men
with weapons which leave a sporting chance of life.
In modern warfare a whole nation is under arms,
and the remaining population of women and children
is in as great, if not greater, danger than the army
in the trenches; towns are undefended, and in a brief
time they can be utterly destroyed from the air and
by bombs and gases which can cause infinite suffering. Such universal suffering, such destruction and
ruin, physical and mental, is out of all proportion
to any possible good which can be won, and, as this

is so, modern war becomes an utterly immoral method for settling disputes.

Such is the argument, and it is a very powerful one. There is, however, an element of exaggeration in it which must be pointed out. The last great war did not leave victor and vanquished in the same plight. England was left with its institutions, and checked what it thought to be unjust aggression. And as to material prosperity, it ill becomes an Englishman to compare the after-effects of the war in his own country with what Germany and Austria, for example, have suffered. Nevertheless, let us grant that a major war between the great nations might have the dire effects prophesied by the pacifist. But it is surely untrue that these effects must follow from all modern wars. There have been a number of minor affrays since the Great War, in Ireland, in China, in South America, in Abyssinia, in North India and at the present moment in Spain. Each may have been destructive to a degree greater than ancient wars—though I doubt it—but some of them have achieved a definite end, and they have not caused universal havoc and collapse. Pacifists such as Bertrand Russell and Aldous Huxley are con- templating a major war, and it is well therefore to distinguish between that and the universal application of the doctrine of non-resistance. In the face of the dread possibility of such a conflagration it would certainly be criminal for any large nation to attempt to embroil the world and to stir up revolutionary strife, or even by diplomatic conversations or preparations to encourage the notion that war was a proper method for settling disputes. Again, to make any use of methods which spread disease and death unnecessarily and by foul means is so immoral as to be diabolical. But alas! the problem is not so simple. The real question arises when such evil courses have been adopted by some nation, or at least when there is every probability that they will be adopted. What is a government to do when it is so threatened? Has it a right to take up defensive measures and so prepare itself that it can meet force with force?

To this I can see only one answer, and that is that until it is much more clearly proved that such defence is not only self-destructive but also destructive of good out of all proportion to any good to be obtained by resistance, no one can call such self-defence immoral. I grant that the just are so handicapped, if they keep to what is morally permitted that they may appear bound to lose. To refuse to use gas and to bomb defenceless cities and with these means paralyse by anticipation an enemy's country, is to invite a massacre of the innocents. That is, indeed, what is said, but the only evidence we have of modern warfare does not appear to make such a result certain, and as in private fighting the fair fighter can still at times defeat the all-in wrestler, and as in business the high code of certain Christian men has not put them entirely at the mercy of unscrupulous rivals, so in war there is still a human factor which counts, and David can still defeat the giant philistine.

To take such a risk, however, and to hold it justifiable there must be the highest and the strongest of motives. Most of the old causes which led to war would no longer justify it, even supposing that they did then, and furthermore the alternative must also be one which is rightly most repugnant to men with deep feelings and enlightened consciences. The pacifist tells us that war never gained mankind anything, and that non-resistance is not only the moral course but also the most successful. That there have been instances when meekness has triumphed is true—and there are also instances when it has not succeeded. The various invasions by the barbarian have destroyed fair civilisations, and on occasions reduced a free people to slavery. The Jews could not rejoice when they were carried off to Babylon and hung up their harps there. The populations under the sway of the Sultans could not be said to enjoy human happiness. How could it be so, when, like the Armenians, they were subject to periodic massacres? It is indeed a strange thing that we should be told in the same breath that to risk life for liberty is man's noblest achievement, and that it is futile and even immoral, that Thermopylae and Ethandune were sordid and of no avail, Kossuth a fool, and Sobieski and Joan of Arc knaves. The pacifists may say that oppression is a thing of the past or that any form of it is more tolerable than war. Mr. Aldous Huxley and Mr. Joad, who incline to this view, are not convincing because they have in mind examples of resolute idealists who are not perturbed by having their hats knocked off or stones thrown at them. What we have to think of is a vast number of people in a state of servitude and of women and children suffering that slow degradation which is part of the technique of the modern tyrant. The bourgeois and many of the peasants in Russia, the Jews in Germany, have had their spirit crushed and all dignity taken from them. And, besides, the violence of man when his passions are aroused is often incited the more by non-resistance, as the

suffering of nuns in Mexico and Spain only too un-
happily proves.

We are mistaken, therefore, if we think that the
alternative to war is a life of peace and in conditions,
humiliating to our pride indeed, but tolerable to
Christians; we have to choose between two horrors,
the one of war and the other of oppression. From
this we can perhaps work out some answers to this
difficult question. War being what it is in modern
times, the words of the present Pope, Pius XI, are
the key to all discussion, that "any nation so mad as
to contemplate war would be guilty of monstrous
homicide and almost certainly of suicide". In those
words are contained the principle and attitude which
should govern national policies, and it means that
any policy which has for its end, direct or indirect,
war, is grossly immoral. There are some Catholic
writers who see in these words a general condemnation of all war, and they back up this belief by
arguing that in the darkness of modern international
politics it is impossible to know who is the aggressor
and who the injured party, and that modern war
is bound of its very nature to be mass murder. No
such general condemnation can be read into the
Pope's words. An issue of such magnitude bearing
immediately on the consciences of all Catholics is

never settled in such a way, and indeed it is difficult to see how the Pope could determine for all cases that a right which varies in different countries and in different circumstances should never be used. The most that we can say is that a large scale war is such that it is almost impossible to think of it as ever justifiable, and that there are bound to be other means of settling a dispute without resorting to universal slaughter. The only exception of which I can think is one so remote as to be at present outside discussion. On two hypotheses, one that the forces of international atheism were to become so large so united and so militant as to wish to thrust their theory on the rest of the world by arms, the second that the remaining States were so loyal to the religious and moral traditions of Christendom as to unite to withstand these forces, on these two hypotheses war might be the only choice the latter could adopt.

The same objections do not apply in the same degree to a small-scale war, though again the strongest of reasons is necessary to make it justifiable. Certainly no one can charge the conscience of those who refuse to tolerate slavery or, what may be worse than that, the loss of all that they hold dear, family, country and religion, and accuse them of sin. That would be in the name of a pacifism which is doubtful to deprive persons of the right to resist to the death what is to them worse than death. The Carlists of Navarre are fighting for what they think the holiest of causes, the defence of their faith and their country's traditions against a foe whose avowed aim is to abolish what they love. Some causes mean more to men than suffering or death, and for this love and the welfare of those who are to come after them they are prepared to thrust back the infidel or die in the attempt. This attitude has immemorially been acclaimed by mankind and held in high honour by Christian men, and in the conditions which I have mentioned their actions are not immoral but righteous.

Lastly, there is the question of the Christian view of non-resistance. The evidence of the Christian attitude in the first centuries can be found put very concisely in the booklet already mentioned, *A Primer of Peace and War*. Mr. Aldous Huxley, in his pamphlet on constructive peace, quotes some early Christian writers to prove the mind of Christianity, and cites the teaching of Christ in favour of pacifism. That there is a strain in the Gospels which is pacifist and that in the early Church there was hesitation among its writers is undoubted. The facts are, how-

ever, that from the beginning Christians seem to
have served in the Roman army, and Christ himself
never chided a soldier for wearing a military uni-
form. In this problem, as in so many others, we are
struck by that extraordinary practical wisdom of
the Church which allows it to be realist without
compromise. The authentic interpretation of Christ's
doctrine became gradually clearer and it cannot be
discovered by reliance on one single text. A critic
of Dr. Temple, the Archbishop of York, was able
to make a score against him by remarking that his
Christianity consisted in contradicting Christ. The
critic was referring to the text, which bids us not
to resist evil, and by this sneer at Dr. Temple he no
doubt impressed many. But such methods of con-
troversy are quite unfair. The mind of Christ can be
learnt from many texts and contexts, and the ideal
preached by Christ has been consistently practised
down the ages. In Russia, in Mexico, in Spain, those
who have freed themselves from temporal responsibilities and devoted themselves purely to spiritual
interests have displayed that gospel meekness which
the pacifist expects from all Christians. The early
Christians in their position of aloofness from the
concerns of the Pagan Empire of which they were
subjects, and vividly conscious of the spiritual king-

dom of Christ, were inclined theoretically to distinguish too sharply between the two kingdoms, as if all Christians belonged to a religious order. But they reached out to the temporal kingdom in their insistence on loyalty and obedience to the ruling power and they allowed Christians to take their part in the State and to serve in its army. When the time came when they had to take up civic responsibilities more frequently and became more conscious of the interrelation of the two kingdoms they became aware of the full meaning and practice of Christ, and St. Augustine and others worked out the complete theology.

Christ, as victim and High Priest of the world and Lord of the Kingdom He came to establish, Himself set the example which His followers dedicated to His service must follow. He was led as a lamb to the slaughter and opened not His mouth. All who are Christians are bound to aim at the same charity and meekness, and unless there are other grounds and other obligations they should do their best to love their enemies by non-resistance. I say that they are bound to aim at the same charity, not that this perfect life is imposed on them under penalty of sin. As human persons each and everyone has a right by nature to protect himself and demand justice,

and the new commandment of Christ does not override the fundamental rights of man. The Christian
remains a moral man if he resists unjust aggression,
but he is invited by Christ to act perfectly by the
standard of the new kingdom, namely, charity, and
even if he does not respond to this completely, he
must at least when acting within his rights motivate
his act by charity. It is in this way that he sur-
passes those who apparently act like him, and he
is no Christian if there be no charity at all present
in his action and motive. The counsel to non-
resistance falls directly on those who by profession
or vow have separated themselves from the concerns
of this world to take up Christ's spiritual work.
Nuns and priests and religious men do not retaliate
and fight. Having no temporal interests, and no
responsibilities for children and wife, having sur-
rendered their possessions and given up their liberty
to be captives of Christ, they can pay their taxes
and confer many services on their country, but they
are tied by no contracts which should oblige them
to fight and the State should not conscript them for
that purpose.

The layman is not so free of temporal responsibilities. He should have charity in his heart and turn
with the utmost reluctance to the thought of shed-

ding blood. His thoughts should be of peace, and if he be forced to contemplate war it should be in the mood of one who is prepared if need be to sacrifice his life for others, to defend the weak and the oppressed and not to take vengeance or to give vent to fighting instincts. That such sacrifice may still be fruitful and necessary I have tried to show. The example of Spain is there to prove it, for the Christian leaders of Spain have tried for years by constitutional means to avoid war; they have been treated outrageously by the Republic they wished to serve, and it was only after every peaceful means had been tried to save their country from the worst of evils, and when their enemies were preparing to spring a mine of revolution, that they had to resort to arms—and then not for political purposes, nor for self-aggrandisement, but to keep the name of Christ alive in their country and on their children's lips. In this act of self-sacrifice they did not forsake the standard of the Prince of Peace; they knew that there could be no peace where Christ was not allowed to reign; they had seen what militant atheism had meant in other countries, and they were determined by life or death that they would not permit their country to be separated from the source of all its good.

VI

A CRITICISM OF MARX

In his admirable study of Marx, Mr. Christopher Dawson comments on "his union of intense apocalyptic conviction with a materialistic philosophy". These words will be the burthen of what follows. Let me begin with an ancient truism. "On earth the life of man is a warfare." Marx calls it a "dialectic", but we know it better as a conflict between selfishness and unselfishness, indulgence and self-control, or the flesh which lusteth against the spirit. Morally and religiously the contrast is given in the famous words of Augustine: "Two loves built two cities— the earthly, which is built up by the love of self to the contempt of God, and the heavenly, which is built by the love of God to the contempt of self." We have here on a more exalted plane the two forms of a city set forth in Plato's Republic, and what Plato calls the city of swine is described still more uncompromisingly by Augustine. "Earthly kingdoms are founded, not in justice, but in injustice. They are created by the sword, by robbery, cruelty, perjury, craft and fraud. . . . What monarchy is there but began in invasion or usurpation? What revolution has been effected without self will, violence and hypocrisy? What popular government but is blown about by every wind, as if it had no conscience and no responsibilities? What dominion of the few but is selfish and unscrupulous? Where is military strength without the passion for war? Where is trade without the love of filthy lucre, which is the root of all evil?" These words do not seem to me altogether inapplicable as we survey the States of the world at the present day, and they recall, too, something of the passion and some of the conclusions of Marx. They do not, however, represent the final view of Augustine nor the Christian theory of the State, for it is in an intimate interplay and concordance of two principles or cities or strains that peace, the tranquillity of order, in Augustine's definition, is reached. This philosophy of history is one which Marx could not appreciate, born as he was at a time when it was completely ignored. It is less excusable that his disciples should know nothing of it, and be ignorant that there is a Christian philosophy of history to be found in Augustine, Aquinas, Bossuet, de Maistre in part, and the political thought of the anti-liberals and Carlists, Balmez, Viluma and Mella.

My point, however, at the moment is not the development of this philosophy so much as the light it throws on Marx's analysis and doctrine. Assume that both in the individual and in the State the spiritual, the religious, call it what you will, must act as a yeast or as a kind of superlative phronesis if society is to be virtuous and happy, then in the separation of the two and their solitary life will be found failure and something damnable. In the past three hundred years this is what has happened. On the one side a secularist State bent on its own business and on the other, idealists, religious doctrinaires, mystics, and artists, even the philosophers, as Nietzsche describes them, sitting on the steps in the shade out of the rays of the sun and busy stitching and sewing the breeches of the spirit. We have a long line of idealists, Berkeley, Gheulincx, Malebranche, Leibniz on to Hegel, the protagonist of the Idea, and on the other hand the empiricists who become more and more the recording instruments of the flux of sensations and events. At a moment when these two tendencies or strains are starkly separate fling a *déraciné* Jew, with all the high powers of a Jew to pass a judgment, and what will happen?

The answer is the Marxian philosophy or method. Marx is brought up on Hegel; he is outraged by the vacuity of the Idea and the forcing of events into its dewlap or pelican's pouch. Absenting himself therefore from attendance on the Idea he looks around at a world without any logic directing it, and he sees with truth that it is physical needs which dominate life, that Augustine's judgment is right. It is money or lucre, the passport to satisfaction of these needs which is the key to history as he witnessed it. Moreover the satisfaction of these needs is determined. Man when he is content to be ruled by his appetite, when he assimilates himself to the material world, is no longer free in any moral or absolute sense, and so it is that in Marx the old philosophy of fatalism, disguised under the name of determinism, the wheel of necessary change, the inevitable movements of time and destiny, all those dark creatures of ancient paganism, reappear. We know quite well as individuals that interior freedom can only be gained by a discipline which relies on the truth and possibility of self-mastery, and all of us are conscious of the slavery to which the instincts can drag us if we indulge them. The world which Marx saw had indulged its instincts of power and greed, and it is no wonder that Marx should have thought that it was possible to describe men in terms of exploiters and exploited and as the result of economic forces. Of course, in this conclusion he was wrong, as any general conclusion of this sort about a body of human individuals is bound to be. No one, however subhuman much of his behaviour may be, can be treated as a thing or a product of a thing; but nevertheless Marx in so delineating man is nearer to Aquinas than to the idealists. He is looking at a man who has his eyes shut, whereas the idealist will try to walk through a man as if he were not there.

But Marx would never have written a Communist Bible if he had rested content with this portrait of the economic robot. There is a passion for justice and a revolutionary spirit in him which made him in his personal life devoted to a cause which had no heart in it. And it would seem as if it were the Jew in him which is responsible for this. Those who know the Hebrew literature will be aware how resounding is the Messianic and apocalyptic note in it—(The Christian philosophy, I may say, has the same note in a different key and is unintelligible without it)—and the Jew has in his blood the expectation of a change and the hope of salvation, temporal or eternal. If like Marx the Jew is *déraciné* and severed from his own people, his thirst for

162

righteousness and a millenium may rest on the strangest of philosophies and his means be by revolution and violence. There will be, to quote my opening remark again, "the union of intense, apocalyptic conviction with a materialistic philosophy".

It is this combination which helps to explain the inconsistencies and contradictions in Marxism. Historically it is important as writing the epitaph of the pseudo-liberalism which was working itself out in his lifetime. Mr. Stephen Spender has recently written a book urging liberals to become communist. He is right in denouncing this secular liberalism, though he is only now and somewhat confusedly realising what Marx grasped nearly a hundred years ago. Marx had no illusions on the nature of this liberalism. He saw the industrial age in England at its worst and he saw it as an outsider. He had lived as a youth under the reactionary rule of Frederick William III and IV; he had studied a philosophy, the Hegelian dialectic, which seemed to him to give the clue to the cosmic and determinist movement of history. Strauss and Feuerbach had settled for him once and for all the unreality of the Christian religion, and the spectacle of so-called Christian men and women in England living on religious sentiment and supporting the oppression of the poor under the name of a moral and religious liberalism nauseated him. In this judgment he was unfair to many high-minded liberals like Maurice and John Stuart Mill. But his judgment did lay bare the latent hypocrisy of much liberal thought which persisted in this country and still shows itself in the way a comfortable capitalistic class is reacting to Communism and Fascism. Its intellectuals adopt a liberalistic interpretation of Marx, excuse its violence and become its apologists for just the motives and in just the spirit which Marx detested, and at the same time, with what Marx would have dubbed a typical bourgeois mentality, they are shocked at that condition of the poor for which they are responsible and write to the papers about the attacks on liberty in countries not their own.

Marx was astute enough to see that bourgeois society, capitalism and secular liberalism were part of the same thing, and hence his indignation with so many of the contemporary socialist attempts, especially of the liberal intellectuals, to remedy the evils of the poor. He ignored Christianity for the reason I have given. His early education had led him to think that it was dead and that it belonged to feudal society, and what he saw in England did not seem to him to be religion at all. He ignored the sentiment and tried to look at the facts, and we now can agree with him to this extent that the liberalism was essentially secular, that it had achieved its great results by means which were materialistic and not spiritual. Whereas in summing up the Middle Ages we should have to signal out its high speculation, its attempt to co-ordinate Europe under a spiritual ideal, its religious painting and architecture, and such social experiments as that of the Franciscans, in the liberal age, as Marx wrote in the Communist manifesto the "bourgeoisie has subjected the country to the rule of the towns. It has created enormous cities, has greatly increased the urban population as compared with the rural . . . has created more massive and more colossal productive forces than have all preceding generations altogether. Subjection of nature's forces to man, machinery, application of chemistry to industry and agriculture, steam navigation, railways, electric telegraphs, clearing of whole continents for cultivation, canalization of rivers, whole populations conjured out of the ground . . ."—this is what was happening, and he despised the liberal attempt to idealise all this by the use of spiritual and mystical words. The process when the chanting of the liberal intellectuals was over, could be seen to be materialistic and to have

M

at its end revolution and a materialistic society.

While taking the side of Marx in his antagonism to secular liberalism, I must not be thought to ignore the many private, magnificent efforts to alleviate suffering and make a moral society during this period. I believe that Marx was wrong in that he treated human efforts of this kind as unimportant compared with the trend of events. He thought that a philosophy of life arose out of economic conditions; what he should have said was that human beings are strongly affected by their economic conditions, and in the period of liberalism they allowed themselves to be duped by a philosophy of material progress and to think of a passing temptation of man as a lasting philosophy. It is this spiritual mistake which makes the end of the period so tragic, and I would add that it is just because Marx has provided a hard and final solution that many alarmed at last by the painfully sentimental and now decrepit attitude of capitalistic philosophy have been drawn towards it.

What the Christian philosopher with his long memory will know to be a passing and unfortunate heresy against the spirit of man the Liberal now sees as a bourgeois movement which has to be taken up into dialectical materialism. As Dr. Gurian has said: "Marxism, and therefore Bolshevism, does but voice

the secret and unavowed philosophy of the bourgeois society when it regards society and economics
as the absolute. . . . Bolshevism is at once the product of bourgeois society and the judgment upon it.
It reveals the goal to which the secret philosophy of
that society leads if accepted with unflinching logic."

To return to Marx. He took a pride in his detec-
tion of the trend of events which were disguised by
the ideological pretences of bourgeois liberalism. It
may be said that neither his early education nor his
experience in England gave him any reason for
questioning the conclusion he drew. This would be
an exaggeration, as everyone has within him a witness to the falsehood of materialism, and, as I have
said, there was not wanting a certain grandeur in
Victorian England. But he followed most men in
falling in love with their supposedly original ideas,
and Marx as even such a worshipper as his bio-
grapher, Otto Rühle (who gave his bad liver as the
cause!), admits, was a jealous man.

But what has made Marxism such a force and at
the same time such a mass of inconsistencies is the
"union of intense apocalyptic vision with a materialistic philosophy". No materialistic philosophy has
so far been able to withstand destructive criticism,
but apart from the defects inherent in its character

as such there is a radical inconsistency brought about by Marx's Hebrew and prophetic instinct. The philosophic inferences drawn from the conditions of society as he saw it are infused with a prophetic hatred of injustice and a messianic desire to change them catastrophically. Though he affected to despise his own people, he was, like them, always on the march to a promised land, preparing for a kingdom of righteousness. It is this Jewish strain in him which makes him, in accordance with the great Jewish writers, indulge constantly in abstractions and makes him, too, place in the foreground of his prophecies a coming revolution to be succeeded by an era like to a millenium. The result has been that he is in flagrant contradiction with himself, that he is always leaping to false conclusions, that his dialectical materialism consists not of opposites held together in some synthesis but of a suicidal incoherence, and that he handed on to posterity a doctrine of hate, a city of avarice and a final despair.

To begin first with his incidental mistakes. He never asked himself whether he himself with his character would have been happy in the ideal society to come. Rühle, his admirer, described him as not a team worker. "He was not a man of comradely spirit, not one of those whose powers are intensified by the sense of living in community with others. He was not a rank-and-file fighter. He could only create as first in the field; could only fight as generalissimo; could only conquer when assigned the heroic rôle. He was a lonely eagle on an ice-bound crag." There would have to have been ice-bound crags in the sunlit plain of the perfect communistic society! Again, he did not stop to examine his history. His description of the earliest ages of man is mythological; he confuses together the Dark Ages and the Middle Ages, and he ignores the crucial example of his own people, the story of the greatness of Israel, which knocks the bottom out of his theory. The greatness of Israel was not economic; it differed little in that respect from the countries round it. The greatness of the Jews of the Old Testament and the impact of Christianity on history are outside the sphere of economics. What Marx did was to make a hasty generalisation from the conditions and outlook of his time and even in this he erred greatly. He could not see that the actions and theories of contemporary reformers were anything more than sentiment or hypocrisy, and that made him unfair to Mazzini, Lassalle, Bakunin and many others; he never grasped the meaning of the Hegelian system, a pardonable error perhaps, but still a serious one, and what is more strange he could not see that he himself was an anomaly in his own system. Having divided off the bourgeois from the proletarian and laid down that there is no such thing as a good man, but only a good bourgeois or good proletarian, thus setting class interest as the ultimate criterion, he ought to have seen that the only true act of immorality is for a bourgeois or proletarian to betray his class. And yet he is the outstanding example, with Engels, of a man with bourgeois upbringing and of bourgeois class betraying it. He proves on his own theory that he must be a bad proletarian just as he is a bad bourgeois.

The prophetic strain in Marx did not allow him to content himself with analysis and theory. As is well known, he believed only in thought that was on the march to action. Whether this combination is possible I will discuss later. For the moment it is enough to point out some of the unfortunate results of his over-hasty enthusiasm. As a critic has written: "Hence the absurd but telling views that the work of the capitalist entrepreneur has no value, that the organisation of exchange adds no value to commodities and that therefore all "profits" are stolen from the wage earners. Hence the doctrine of ever-increasing misery in spite of the evidence of the facts. Hence the statements of one-sided tendencies preached as though they were the whole story, such as: 'The weapons with which the bourgeoisie overthrew feudalism are now being turned against the bourgeoisie itself'. The workers who are forced to sell themselves piecemeal are a commodity like any other article of commerce, and are consequently exposed to all the vicissitudes of competition. Wages are everywhere forced down to the same level. Hence the appeal to envy and jealousy: 'The proletarian has no property; his relationship to wife and children is utterly different from the family relationships of bourgeois life. . . . The expropriators are expropriated'" and so forth. In writing such comments he was in too great a hurry to watch what was really happening. This made him such a bad prophet. He expected too much from the revolutions in his early lifetime and middle age, and his predictions have not been very happy. Some of his modern followers unable to defend Marxism as a theory claim that it is indispensable as a method, and I suppose they work out the future in terms of it. But as a method of prediction the doctrine of Marx is comparable with the Egyptian pyramids, which incidentally are monuments built with much human labour and having little surplus value. Sorel, for instance, is sprung from the loins of Marx, and from Sorel proceeds Mussolini and national social-ism. Marx never foresaw what dragons were to lie in the path of his successful revolution and how the violence he preached would be turned against him. Nor again was it fitting that the least bourgeois of the nations in Europe should be the first to collapse before the revolution of a few. In an interview which he once gave to an American newspaper in 1871, Marx declared in answer to the question: "Do you expect to succeed soon in England?"—"Sooner than in any other country, for the reason that labour and capital are already organised upon a co-operative system where the work is done by many skilled hands each doing a part, and where all sorts of labour-saving machines are on the farm and in the factory. Labour is already co-operative. It is only necessary to make the profits mutual by dividing them equally among those engaged in it, instead of giving them all to one man. . . . You would say that if capital is thus assisting progress it must be a good thing—a proposition which I do not altogether deny. I look upon the present state of capital as a stage of development, a necessary stage in human pro-gress, which must naturally develop itself into a higher form of perfection, just as a flower must fall to give way to the fruit, or the blade of green spring before the corn can ripen."

You will notice in this quotation how the image from nature suggests that all that has gone before passes of itself and peaceably into the fruit. The image is not a revolutionary one, nor does the praise of the bourgeois achievement fit in with many a passage where stirred with passionate detestation of the iniquity of capitalism, he bids the ruling classes tremble at the prospect of a communist revolution. He was never clear about the way his dialectic worked. In Hegel the idea does genuinely develop. Marx moves uncertainly, seeing at one moment the past moving to its opposite in the future and conserving what was best there, and the next moment he is horrified by the spectacle of the capitalism which devoured the poor, and he determined to end it. Thus in the Communist Manifesto he says that the bourgeois "has accomplished wonders far surpassing Egyptian pyramids, Roman aqeducts and Gothic cathedrals; it has conducted expeditions that put in the shade all former exoduses of nations and crusades". How different, however, is the estimate when he writes: "The civilisation and justice of bourgeois order comes out in its lurid light whenever the slaves and drudges of that order rise against their masters. Then this civilisation and justice stand forth as undisguised savagery and lawless revenge. Each new crisis in the class struggle between the appropriator and the producer brings out this fact more glaringly. Even the atrocities of the bourgeois in June 1848 vanish before the ineffable infamy of 1871." And again, in *Capital* he says that "the history of the colonial administration of Holland, the model capitalist nation during the seventeenth century, is according to Thomas Stamford Raffles, sometime lieutenant-governor of Java, 'one of the most extraordinary relations of treachery, bribery, massacre and meanness' " It is in passages such as these that he becomes the Hebrew prophet hating injustice and calling for a radical change. He is a moralist who unwittingly shows up the nonsense he has written about dialectical materialism. Remember that the only morality he recognises is the morality of the class and that this consists in loyalty to the interests of the class. To an empiricist and Marxist there can be no meaning in the notion of human equality. Visibly men and women differ in body and brains, and we can never verify our belief in equality. It may be called a mystical—what I would call a reasonable metaphysical and religious— view, for which above all Christianity is responsible;

but it has no place in Marxism. Marxists are indeed always ill at ease with it. Mr. Strachey tells us that the real doctrine concerns the distribution in the socialist State of products in accordance with the value of individuals' work, and in the Communist State with the needs of the recipients. I doubt whether these two programmes can be made to look reasonable without some doctrine of equality in the background, and at any rate they raise so many difficulties in the administration of a perfect society that no one has yet been able to work out how this programme could be realised. We have no means for testing ability and no agreed scale of the relative importance of needs and their satisfaction, and as no one is a good judge of himself in this matter we must be handed over to a dictator for him to settle. But the Marxist cannot afford to dispense with the ideal of equality; he has to use it to win followers, and he will be powerless to inveigh against injustice and present conditions unless he believes in it. Marx had always before his mind the emancipation of the proletariat and a classless State, and how much equality and fraternity meant to him is brought out in his Address to the International Working Man's Association in 1865. Here we read "that the emancipation of the working classes must be conquered by the working classes themselves; that the struggle for the emancipation of the working classes means, not a struggle for class privileges and monopolies, but for equal rights and duties and the abolition of all class rule. That the economic subjection of the man of labour to the monopolizer of the means of labour, that is, the sources of life, lies at the bottom of servitude in all its forms, of all social misery, mental degradation and political independence. . . ."

It will be noticed here how almost all of Marx's words are winged with moral fervour. It may be said that as morality, in his view, extends as far as class loyalty, and is defined and limited by that, such fervour is justified. This defence will not hold water for a moment, for the words imply that as a class they are suffering from injustice and that their state should be changed into one more just. He is indicting once more the oppressors and inciting the proletariat to revolt against them. He has in mind the wrongdoing of the capitalists and bourgeois as exploiters of the poor by means of "treachery, bribery massacre and meanness". And yet on his own standards they are entirely moral in doing their utmost in the interests of their class. Whatever interpretation we put upon these moral views of Marx, the result is horrible. If we cling to the doctrine that class morality is what he meant and nothing else, then we see in a new form the pernicious old idea of nationalism as an absolute. We have learnt to our cost the danger of a State or nation claiming that morality is identical with its will. That a class should do so makes no ultimate difference. Both involve a denial of our common humanity and degrade the notions of truth and justice, and we are back in the false imperialism which could commit atrocities in the Congo and treat lesser races outside the law as slaves and beasts of burden. This seems to be the orthodox interpretation of Marxism as it has been taught by the outstanding Marxists of the present era. It is their express declaration that "we do not recognise any other moral save the choice of means which will best lead the strife we are engaged in to its successful completion". The view, it may be added, is in accordance with the principles of Marx in as much as he lays it down that ideas are nothing more than the reflection of the economic interests of the time. Hence it follows that just as the capitalist was said to excuse his exploitation by moral maxims taken from his desires or by hypocritically disguising them, so too the proletariat must have a morality which represents and rationalises its revolutionary and sanguinary methods.

Naturally the Messianic Marx did not realise that he was in fact denying all morality and justifying every form of misery and oppression. To him in this mood the proletariat were the host of Israel. They are endowed with all the virtues; they will exhibit all the glory of man and bring about a millenium where no human weakness or vice will be discernible. No empirical or materialistic generalisation could possibly guarantee that the last State of society will be an improvement on any other; that one class can be called blessed and that a communistic State will live in peace and harmony. A topsy-turvy religious or mystic belief has here taken charge of Marx's thought, and he never questioned it, any more than he questioned the absolute truth of his own doctrine. On his own principles his views should have been just the reflection of the economic situation and entirely relative to it. They should have been dismissed with the same contempt with which he dismissed the beliefs and philosophies of the bourgeois and all that was not determined by the immediate situation. What he chose to think was that he had uttered the final word on the story of the world and had unmasked the processes of history which had always until his time been misunderstood. And in their admiration for their master many of his disciples have made the same mistake. It is illuminating to find, for instance, one of them describing Marx in terms which belong only to a spiritual philosophy. "He became the saviour of humanity at large and built for eternity."

It is now time to look more closely into the chief doctrines of Marx. I have already laid emphasis on the double rôle which Marx played, as the economist and materialist philosopher and the revolutionary and apocalyptic visionary. The combination of both in one system led to continual contradiction and has made the task of interpreters a hard one. As is well known there has been a variety of interpretations. The chief claimants to his name have been Engels, the German social democrats, the school of Bernstein or revisionists, the syndicalists led by Sorel, and the Bolsheviks. Most would now say that the latter are nearest to Marx, or at least were so when Lenin was alive. But it must be admitted that the other interpreters had grounds for their belief. Engels, for instance, who spent a life of such noble devotion to the interests of Marx and knew him as no one else, came more and more to regard the work of Marx as a system, scientific and philosophic, and only secondarily as a method of revolution. He puts together a theory of knowledge out of his master's writings, a theory which makes knowledge identical with sensations. How such a knowledge can be a force and serve in a dialectic is not clear. But then the fact that Marx himself both held this and also made knowledge active does not make the mystery of how these two could go together any the clearer. Kautsky, Hilferding and others preferred to concentrate on the scientific side of Marxism, and in their hands it became an explanation of how history had come to pass rather than a method for making history. This caricature, as the revolutionaries thought it, was dubbed "astronomical Marxism", and the emphasis, right or wrong, on the scientific character of *Capital* can be seen in the statement of Rudolf Hilferding that "Marxism is only a theory of the laws of movement of society formulated in general terms by the Marxian conception of history; the Marxian economics applying in particular to the period of commodity production." Bernstein in turn lifted the theory on to a moral plane. Being a neo-Kantian in outlook he saw that the relativist morals proclaimed by Marxists around him were fatal to the system. Class dictatorship meant not a social progress but a relapse into barbarism, and class violence implied the denial of the rights of other classes as human beings. In this revision of the orthodox doctrine the place of violence was taken by peaceable progress and evolution. That such a revision was necessary if the dialectic was to hold water and the moral fervour of Marx to be consistent, there can be no doubt. On the other hand, class violence and revolution are of the very essence of Marx, and in scouting the peaceable ideas of the revisionists and returning to this, Sorel was also faithful to Marx. Sorel has often been abused for "decomposing Marx", but this is an unjust accusation, as he meant by this phrase the false, as he thought, interpretations of Marx which had grown up, and he always regarded himself as the true heir of the Marxist doctrine. In contrast with parliamentarism and social democracy he glorified violence and bothered little about the theory. As again it is an inherent part of Marxism that ideas are but the intellectual shadow cast by economic movements, it is difficult to see that he was wrong. The blame lies with Marx, who could hand down so many conflicting ideas. The last form of Marxism is represented by Lenin. This school is too well known to need description. It succeeded and thus justified Marx as no theorist could do, and as it bothered little about contradictions so long as the immediate aim was successfully accomplished, it can with justice be said to be a repetition of all the inconsistencies and confusions of Marxism.

It is undeniable that each of the schools I have mentioned used some part of Marx's doctrine and tried to be logical. Marxism does contain a theory and that theory Marx thought to be the one and only scientific account of history. It was also a method and as a method did not worry about theory except in so far as the theory led to action. That there is no standard of morality in the method is clear from passage after passage which could be cited from Marx, but at the same time the great conception of Marx was to him vividly a moral one, and all the power and persuasion contained in it as a method depend on a moral stimulus. Hence we are in the presence of contradictions of all sorts, and the only way out, it would seem, is to cast the theory on one side and make a practical experiment of its method. But what is this method? When scrutinised it disappears and becomes theory, and it cannot serve as a programme of revolt and a scheme of universal emancipation and happiness towards which the proletariat should aim. It must make a claim to be true, and if it does this then it cannot escape the criticism of it as a doctrine. The Marxist may say that in science there have been many hypotheses which have been invented simply for the sake of simplifying experience and making headway, and again that in medical science a course of treatment may be used about the theoretical value of which we may know next to nothing. Indeed psycho-analysis lives on myth, and nevertheless is justified by its occasional successes. This might do if it were true that Marxism were a mere economic *ad hoc* method, recognised by all who use it as a possibly useful means of explaining the course which econo-mics tends to take. I have shown (and the economists who have lectured on the subject have shown) that the method is out of date and its predictions con-stantly belied, but that is not all. A practical science which by definition is an abstraction from the total situation must assume that that what it leaves out is true and unaffected by its method. If we take a subject such as ethics, which treats of human con-duct, we cannot neglect the theoretical side. That is to say, whereas a practical science may proceed as if results were the sole test of its truth, a philo-sophic view cannot do this, since it is concerned with what is ultimate and already known. If we already know that man is a rational animal we cannot take as a method what assumes him to be an irra-tional animal. We should then be trying to explain ethics by what was just not ethics. Marxism can never be content to be a manual of economics written half a century ago and therefore out of date. Society would not be disturbed by such, nor kingdoms uprooted. Marx meant in all he said and did that his dialectical materialism was to be taken seriously, and he was convinced that he had exposed the nature of man and the nature of history. Man was nothing more than a tool-working animal determined by the nature of his tool and inspired by the tool to deal with it in a certain way and so improve the tool and his surroundings. This is a picture of a beaver but not a human being, and just as a beaver will fight ruthlessly against an alien species and in defence of its progeny, so man docketed in a class must fight ruthlessly for his own interests and for the interests of his class, and that is the full tale of morality.

Marxism as a philosophy and as a method is in contradiction, and furthermore if taken as a philosophy it is manifestly false, and as a method it has been superseded. It is legitimate for the sake of determining by experiment the degree of its truth to consider man as economic or as sexual or as influenced by the four humours. The value of such a method will vary with the age and types of men, but the method of Marx has, in fact, done very little to enlighten us. I have heard Marx defended by a modern Communist on the ground that he showed us that material and economic motives played a large part in human life. For such a common-place truth we did not need the vast structure of Marxism. As a philosophy it has not the merits of the more carefully thought out systems of materialism. I have said that it rests on an inverted Hegelianism. Many of us do not think that Hegel found the key to truth, but at least Hegel deserves to be understood. Marx says: "my dialectic method is in principle not only different but directly opposed to that of Hegel. For Hegel the spiritual process which he goes so far as to transform into an independent subject under the name of the Idea, is the demiurge of reality, and reality is only its exterior manifestation." This is quite false. Reality in Hegelianism is not the exterior of the Idea but its content. So Marx preserves of the Hegelian system only the notion of opposites, and he means by that principle strife considered as a principle of development. All that this comes to is that a negative force sets society going and governs its different phases, and this negative force is the class struggle. Materialism in a dialectic of class struggle, there is the philosophy of Marx.

As an explanation of history its only evidence is the present struggle. Antiquity does not supply us with any decisive information on the subject of a class struggle, but all the evidence we have suggests that a simple explanation by class strife would be anachronistic and absurd. The future, too, is to be without a class struggle, and not all the efforts of zealous Marxists can avail to explain away this contradiction in the Marxian dialectic. Either the class struggle is just an empirical generalisation with some support at the present time and a support which fades the further we go back in history or it is the warp and woof of history, a truth which is the very soul of the Marxian system. On the first horn lies dead all that goes to make Marx important; on the second is exposed the manifest untruth of the dialectic in its final stage. Moreover, what is this class struggle about? Marx explains it in terms of tools and production; but these suppose that human beings are dissatisfied, and unless we know the source of this dissatisfaction we are left without anything but an empty form of explanation. Is it physical misery? Physical needs are certainly causes of effort and at times of strife, but usually violence does not take place until the misery is thought of as unjust. Struggles can be of all kinds, and dissatisfaction is responsible for all manner of changes. To call all these by the name of a class struggle is like calling all exercise and play by the name of team work.

And how in this conflict does something new appear? If the dialectic is to enlighten us the change ought to be of one pattern, but no one can tell us what precisely is the nature of this change. Certain scientific philosophers, struck with the apparent fact that in combinations of physical elements something new resulted, coined the phrase Emergent Evolution to cover this fact. It is not easy to see how evolution which ought to be continuous can at the same time be an emergence into something really novel, and for a similar reason it is difficult to see how materialism can be at the same time dialectical. It looks as if the authors of these descriptions thought that by putting two incoherent words together they had somehow managed to lessen the incoherence. The word "dialectical" has a meaning in Hegel because it describes originally a method of discussion, and therefore can be used of the process of thought. But to transfer it to a material process is to plunge us into darkness. Some defenders of it try to give parallels from physical changes of the kind already mentioned, when something new comes forth. So then what happens is that "dialectical" which was used to describe the movement of thought or discussion is transferred to a change in matter, and then this change in matter which only by a metaphor can be called dialectical is used to explain how the word dialectical can appropriately be applied to historical change! Leaving aside the obvious difference that a chemical change can be repeated whereas an historical change cannot, we are still left ignorant of what happens in this historical change. Is what precedes destroyed or is it preserved, and if preserved is all preserved or only part? And again, is this part or whole preserved unchanged or changed, and if changed, in what way changed? The examples which Marx gives seem to cover all varieties, and if this is so, all that the dialectical process means is that in change the result is not the same as what went before.

Marx calls his system, dialectical materialism. It should be noted that the substantive is materialism. There are many idealists and intellectuals who forget this, and carried away by humanitarian, or religious ideals they proceed to read into Marx their own desires and to count themselves his followers. A recent series of articles in the *Spectator* on Communism showed liberals and Christians trying to coax the doctrine of Marx into the Apostle's Creed or Sermon on the Mount. Mr. Middleton Murry sublimates materialism into his own religious vision of the future, and Professor Macmurray finds room in the dialectic of Marx for a religion of purely human relations based on love. Such a love mankind has always in its best moments desired, but it has no bearing on a dialectic which begins with matter and ends with matter. Marxists are never tired of telling us that their materialism is in no sense the physical materialism of nature, that it includes brains and human thought and will. It might be unfair to point out how despite this they constantly seek to find parallels in physical nature, and how some of them have worked out a system which stretches from the dialectic of atoms to the history of philosophy. Let us grant that neither Marx nor Marxism is committed to crude materialism. We have definite explanations on which to rely. Marx tells us, for instance, that "labour is above all an act which is the joint product of man and nature; man in face of nature plays the rôle of a natural force." The physical movement of his body and his members directed by intelligence makes of matter something useful to the body; it is thus the maker of history. The fact that we are capable of changing nature proves that we have knowledge of external nature, and this is always taken for granted in dialectical materialism. If we could not grasp its meaning, then the development of technique, the discovery of machines and all the labour of man would be a chimera. It is from these principles that Marx works out his economic history.

It would be easy to show the extraordinary character of the assumption that we have this complete knowledge of nature, but it is more relevant to comment on the special form which this materialistic theory takes. Material changes determine man's activity, and as man co-operates in the making of the tool and the machine, he, too, with his will and intelligence can be said to be active in history. But first, can the making of a tool or machine be called a material event at all? As Mr. Wood has written: "The history of tools is essentially part of the intellectual and spiritual life of mankind. Their invention and use are determined by the mind. In a mechanistic universe a mechanical invention would be impossible and indeed inconceivable. Every tool is a triumph of mind over matter and not, as Professor Levy incautiously asserts, 'a triumph of matter over matter'—a perfect example of a meaningless statement." In joining this activity of will and intellect with the determinism of material conditions Marx is running with the hare and hunting with the hounds. Dialectical materialism is inherently contradictory. We cannot hold that man is ultimately determined by the historical, economic material situation and at the same time really determining it by his will and mind. Either one triumphs or the other; that both should do so is impossible. Marxism in its literal interpretation therefore means that the intelligence of man is determined, that he is not free, that anything which is beyond an intelligent animal's reaction to its environment must be dismissed as dreamland. For that reason Marx is so scathing in his reference to the intellectuals, and any movement of thought, whether religious, artistic or philosophical, which lifts itself above economic determination. For a similar reason he scoffs at any form of morality which is not effective in producing the economic change which his method of dialectical materialism demands. It is perfectly just therefore to paraphrase Marx's own descriptions of his man of history, and to say that he is defined as a being essentially and exclusively material, whose nature and value consist in making instruments of production and satisfying his primary material needs, eating, sleeping and begetting. Man is an animal and only superior in degree to the rest of the animal kingdom. This superiority consists in his ability to make tools, and his exceptional misery comes from the conflict which necessarily follows from this and forces men into classes, the classes of the exploiter and the exploited. That in this system man should have no private life, no personal dignity, that violence should be a watchword and greed a consuming motive, that immoralities of the most bestial kind should be condoned if they serve the immediate economic end desired, all these conclusions follow inevitably from the premises.

To conclude then. Neither as a philosophy nor as a system can Marxism stand criticism. As a theory it is based on ephemeral evidence and it leaves out all that has made human nature estimable. We have seen enough of the effects of violence since the days of Marx to doubt its efficacy as an offensive in any cause, and we have seen enough impoverishment of thought and ideal not to desire that everything worth while in life should be removed. Marx saw Augustine's "city of avarice" in which the rich prospered, and in such a way that their power must pass into the hands of the labouring classes. He took the lowest estimate of human nature, and he assumed that what the rich sought must be the source of

happiness—as if riches ever brought happiness to
the soul of man!—and his method was apocalyptic-
ally to transfer the power to the masses and bring
them the calm of possession by violence. He chose
the city which can never be at peace, which is
materialised by avarice and is the slave of its cupidi-
ties—a city of despair. He failed to realise this because the old Jewish prophetic zeal swept him away.
The Christian philosophy also believes in an apocalyptic and Messianic kingdom, but that kingdom
was never meant to replace the world empires nor
were the best Christian thinkers milleniarists. In the
Augustinian doctrine of history something new
works itself out in time and disturbs human calcu-
lations. Secular historians and philosophers are per-
vaded by the sense of the inevitable in history, the
law of Drasanti pathein and pathein mathos, the
growing darkness or the coming night. This is the
despair of all secular creeds, the unimportance of
individuals, the fatal trend of events, the wheel of
necessity, the dialectic of Marx. "What", says Croce
—no apologist for Christianity—"are our histories of
culture, of civilisation, of progress, of humanity, of
truth, save the form of ecclesiastical history in harmony with our times—that is to say, of the triumph
and propagation of the faith, of the strife against the

powers of darkness, of the successive treatments of the new evangel made afresh with each succeeding epoch?" In the period preceding Marx this doctrine of the city of God had slipped its moorings and become a vague shape or spectre. Everything in Marx's lifetime led him, as I have already said, to misunderstand the real problem of his period. The two loves which made two cities have expressed themselves in every age, though there is only one authentic account of them, and we know from our own interior experiences and the conflict there of freedom and servitude that this is the dialectic or dialogue present throughout history. In the eighteenth and nineteenth centuries the two loves had become almost hopelessly confused. The Enlightenment saw the liberals assigning to themselves the honour of being the apostles of the higher kingdom. They dreamt dreams the while they encouraged by their philosophy the translation of liberty into license and free men into economic slaves. The Idealists of this period thought they were the heralds of the Kingdom of God, and the scientists turned to an empirical and deterministic theory of nature which grew more and more materialistic. Marx coming upon the scene was naturally led wrong. A Jew by race and Protestant by form he had all the thwarted impulses of the ghetto and hatred of the smug superiority of the Gentile surviving in him. The emancipation and admission of the Jews into bourgeois society prevented him from returning to the Jewish apocalyptic vision, but it could not prevent him from being fiercely hostile to the bourgeois society and mentality. The idealism which had been equated with the higher love and city, the Jewish Messianic kingdom, was to him a soft form of bourgeois sentiment—and he was partly right. All his attention was therefore turned on the life around him, and he traced its sources to the love of cupidity, an inexorable servitude of the spirit to the bodily appetites. He removed the residual idealism, the false claims of the liberals and capitalists to be the children of the enlightenment. At the same time the bourgeois, as Christopher Dawson points out, took the place of the Gentiles, and the economic poor, the proletariat, took the place of the spiritual poor of the Old Testament. The result was contradictory. Into the cold logic of his theory of determinism and the conflict of classes burst the old moral and spiritual frenzy transforming the theory into something revolutionary which would end once for all—let the dialectic be what it may—the long oppression of God's poor and the age of injustice, the reign of the city of avarice and strife. Thus by strife would he end strife, and by determinism bring freedom, and by hatred and avarice peace and fraternity, and by materialism the kingdom of the spirit which Israel had for so long expected. As Dawson so rightly says, "the ultimate verdict on Communism will be that the house it is building for the new humanity is not a palace but a prison, since it has no windows." The answer does not lie there, but in a different revolution, self-inflicted and made possible by the vision of a Man at war with the world and triumphing on a Cross.

MADE AND PRINTED IN GREAT BRITAIN
AT THE BOWERING PRESS, PLYMOUTH